DISABILITY AND DIVERSITY: A SOCIOLOGICAL PERSPECTIVE

DISABILITY AND DIVERSITY: A SOCIOLOGICAL PERSPECTIVE

MARK SHERRY

Nova Science Publishers, Inc.

New York

NOTICE TO THE READER

The Publisher has taken reasonable care in the preparation of this book, but makes no expressed or implied warranty of any kind and assumes no responsibility for any errors or omissions. No liability is assumed for incidental or consequential damages in connection with or arising out of information contained in this book. The Publisher shall not be liable for any special, consequential, or exemplary damages resulting, in whole or in part, from the readers' use of, or reliance upon, this material. Any parts of this book based on government reports are so indicated and copyright is claimed for those parts to the extent applicable to compilations of such works.

Independent verification should be sought for any data, advice or recommendations contained in this book. In addition, no responsibility is assumed by the publisher for any injury and/or damage to persons or property arising from any methods, products, instructions, ideas or otherwise contained in this publication.

This publication is designed to provide accurate and authoritative information with regard to the subject matter covered herein. It is sold with the clear understanding that the Publisher is not engaged in rendering legal or any other professional services. If legal or any other expert assistance is required, the services of a competent person should be sought. FROM A DECLARATION OF PARTICIPANTS JOINTLY ADOPTED BY A COMMITTEE OF THE AMERICAN BAR ASSOCIATION AND A COMMITTEE OF PUBLISHERS.

LIBRARY OF CONGRESS CATALOGING-IN-PUBLICATION DATA

Sherry, Mark, 1971-
  Disability & diversity : a sociological perspective / Mark Sherry.
     p. cm.
  ISBN 978-1-60456-914-8 (softcover)
  1. Disability studies. 2. Sociology of disability. 3. People with disabilities--Social conditions. I. Title. II. Title: Disability and diversity.
  HV1568.2.S535 2008
  305.9'08--dc22
                              2008025044

Published by Nova Science Publishers, Inc. ✦ New York

DEDICATION

This one goes out to the one I love, Molly.

Thank you for your love, attention, kindness, sense of humor, patience, energy and interest   And thank you for being the best research assistant, sounding board, friend, supporter, and lover anyone could have.

CONTENTS

ACKNOWLEDGMENTS

This book began as a series of lectures which I prepared for a class on Disability and Diversity at The University of Toledo. Students responded positively to it, and I decided to revise it and publish it because there were no comparable books on the topic which combined a critical sociological perspective with one informed by the debates of disability studies. I want to thank those students for their interest in the information and their positive feedback, which inspired me to publish it. The book retains some of its origins as a pedagogical tool; nevertheless it is a useful contribution to the literature, I think, because it provides a great deal of information in a fairly accessible format, while still addressing many of the debates that continue to exist in disability studies, medical sociology, and public health.

I want to acknowledge some of the people whose work has touched me deeply. I would like to begin by mentioning my mentor, Professor Susan Schweik from The University of California at Berkeley. She so inspired and influenced me during my Post-Doctoral Fellowship at Berkeley, that I was motivated to jump into a body of literature I'd not previously read in detail. A casual reference to a certain author, or a new book, over a cup of coffee helped me develop a reading list, and a sense of the landscape in Northern American disability studies. I could not imagine someone more supportive of a person who came from another country and seemed so ignorant of many leading authors here. I will be eternally grateful to Susan Schweik. When I write, there is always a little part of my brain thinking "I wonder what Sue would think of this".

I also want to thank others in Disability Studies at Berkeley – particularly Dr. Devva Kasnitz, who warmly welcomed me when I'd only been in America a short time and allowed me to stay in her house as I moved to Berkeley. Wow. That act of kindness alone says a lot about Devva as a remarkable, kind and caring person.

But stories of Devva's personal kindness should not divert one's attention from her formidable intellectual presence. It was Devva, and her colleague Dr. Russell Shuttleworth, who really showed me the incredible contributions of anthropologists to the field of Disability Studies.

My dear friend and colleague Dr. Beth Omansky also contributed enormously to my thinking on disability. Whether we were discussing feelings of alienation that stemmed from a disability hierarchy or the lack of class analysis among many disability studies scholars, or just chatting about the daily experiences of life as a disabled person, Beth always had something interesting and thought-provoking to say. Thank you Beth!

I also want to also thank the graduate students who I worked with at The University of Illinois at Chicago, especially Eunjung Kim, Michael Gill, Michelle Jarman and Sara Vogt. We had such great conversations for the year I was with you – I am really proud to know you all, and I am glad that you all have such great insights, ethics and principles. I felt stimulated and energized by your commitment to rigorous critical scholarship.

I would like to thank Maralyn Klar for her help in Toledo. Keep up the great work, Mazza!

My own thinking was shaped profoundly by my involvement in Australian disability circles. I would like to specially appreciate the work of disability advocacy organizations like Speaking Up For You, Queensland Advocacy Inc., the Community Resource Unit, and Queensland Parents of People with a Disability. This work is very American – it has to be, given that the distribution of disease/illness/disability changes from country to country - but the principles of committed advocacy that you all live by helped to keep me going while I was writing it. And a special thank you to Ken Aitken for your wisdom, insight and your humor.

Thanks to Lesley Chenoweth, my Ph.D. supervisor and another mentor. More than anyone I know, you have shown me how great an ally can be in the disability field. And to my mate Eric, or Dr. Wing Hong Chui as he is more formally known. I miss you, and wish we were still working at a place where we could have coffee every day.

Thanks to my family, for their support across the seas. It's hard being so far away from you!

And once again, thanks to Molly, who sat up night after night with me while I wrote this. I couldn't have done anything without you. Emotionally, physically, and intellectually... you complete me. You had me at hello! You've made my life so much better – my health, my happiness, my outlook, everything. We face the world together so much better, as a couple, than we do as two individuals. As for the future... it's just you and me babe; a deal's a deal.

PREFACE

The book, which is rich in both sociological analysis and in practical analyses, highlights the social, cultural, and politcal factors that portray that some social groups experience disabilities more often than others. It also highlights the barriers that particular groups face in trying to address their medical needs. These difficulties can range from problems with insurance to language problems in dealing with health professionals, or even sexism in medicine. The book also contains many suggestions for reforming health care practices and policies to improve service delivery.

There are five chapters in this book. The first chapter discusses the ideas of disability and diversity, and gives a broad introduction to the topic. This is designed to stimulate the interest of readers, to expose them to some of the ways in which people with disabilities have very diverse experiences, and to demonstrate the importance of recognizing diversity within the disability community.

The second chapter addresses the interaction of ethnicity and disability. As this chapter has already suggested, many ethnic groups experience disproportionate levels of particular disabilities. The chapter outlines some of these disabilities, and also identifies the particular disabling barriers which may arise from this intersection of ethnicity and disability. Of course, recognizing diversity means that we will make an effort to discuss many different ethnic groups in this discussion. This includes those disabilities more common among Caucasians as well as those more common among ethnic minorities in the US.

The third chapter of the book focuses on gender and disability. It emphasizes the ways gender impacts on disability – not just in terms of the ways men and women have different rates of different disabilities, but also some of the ways in which these gender differences create different social and economic opportunities for disabled men and women.

The fourth chapter of the book will discuss the relationship between disability and socioeconomic status. Poorer people have higher rates of many disabilities, and they also have fewer resources to deal with it. So this is an important social justice and public health issue. On the other hand, certain disabilities occur more frequently among people from higher socioeconomic groups, and the chapter will examine those experiences as well.

The book's conclusion, Chapter Five, summarizes the arguments of the book, reinforces the importance of identifying the practical implications of this data, and identifies a number of areas for further research.

Each chapter contains policy and practice recommendations as well as a sociological examination of the interaction of disability with particular demographic categories. The chapters identify particular disabling barriers that exist because of the interaction of disability with demographic factors such as ethnicity, socioeconomic status, gender and age.

Chapter 1

DISABILITY AND DIVERSITY

Sociological perspectives on disability, illness and diversity emphasize the social, cultural, and political factors which influence the incidence of disability, as well as the responses to disability. Such factors may include the interaction of disability with socioeconomic status, age, gender, sexuality, and geographic location. This introductory chapter will highlight some of these factors, which will be explored in more detail in some of the later chapters. Before discussing such factors, however, it is important to define the key terms – "disability" and "diversity".

DISABILITY

Within sociological literature, two competing definitions of disability are dominant. The first definition is one that stems from the medical model of disability, as well as some disability legislation and governmental policies. In this settings, disability tends to be defined very broadly – it can include any physical, cognitive, intellectual, appearance or sensory impairment, or other medical condition that limits a person's major daily activities. Versions of such an approach towards disability can often be found in legislation such as the Americans with Disabilities Act (ADA). From this perspective, disability can include someone who:

- Uses a wheelchair, cane because of a spinal cord injury;
- Has a developmental disability (a disability acquired at birth);
- Is labeled "mentally retarded";

- Has burns all over their face;
- Has an autoimmune disease;
- Has a respiratory disease such as Asthma or Chronic Bronchitis;
- Is blind or has a vision impairment;
- Lives with constant pain;
- Is Deaf or is hard of hearing;
- Has cancer;
- Has AIDS;
- Has seizures;
- Has Carpel Tunnel Syndrome;
- Has Autism or Asperger's syndrome;
- Has a mental illness such as Obsessive Compulsive Disorder;
- Has Chronic Fatigue Syndrome;
- Has a learning disability such as dyslexia;
- Has Attention Deficit/Hyperactivity Disorder;
- Has dyslexia;
- Has Alzheimer's disease; and so on…

All these experiences indicate that a very large group of people experience disability. Some estimates suggest that one in five people has a disability (Russell, 1998). Importantly, however, courts have decided that disability must be defined on a case-by-case basis. This has meant that there is often a legal battle over the severity and extent of an individual's experiences of disability (O'Brien, 2004). Another aspect of the definition of the definition of disability in the ADA is that a person is "disabled" if they are *regarded* (correctly or incorrectly) as having a disability. For instance, someone who is regarded as having a mental illness (but who does not actually have one) might be discriminated against, because of this perceived disability. Such discrimination would be regarded as unlawful under the ADA.

The vast majority of disabilities do not occur at birth. One estimate is that only 15% of people with disabilities are born with them (Shapiro, 1994). This means that the experiences which people commonly define as disability – such as blindness, deafness or cerebral palsy – are actually a small percentage of the overall number of disability. Far more common are those disabilities which tend to occur after birth, such as Alzheimer 's disease, Spinal Cord Injury, Stroke, or Osteoporosis.

A second definition of disability is associated with the social model of disability. This approach suggests that "disability" is not about difference – as human beings, we are all different. Instead, it suggests that the process of defining someone as "disabled" reflects the ways in which societies respond to the rich tapestry of human variation that makes up the human race. Therefore, from this perspective, disability is about *social reactions* to human difference (Sherry, 2006). It's all about what society makes of the physical, cognitive, sensory and mental differences we encounter. Typically, societies are unresponsive to the flexible needs of people with disabilities, who then experience many physical, attitudinal and social barriers. Some scholars who rely on a social model of disability label define these barriers as "disability", rather than the individual impairments people experience (Oliver, 1996).

Unfortunately, a degree of confusion may result from these competing meanings of the term "disability". In order to avoid such problems, this book will rely on the standard (albeit medicalized) definition of disability, and will use the term "disabling barriers" to highlight the barriers which may limit the rights and freedoms of people with disabilities. The advantage of distinguishing between these two competing notions of disability is that it facilitates a sociological examination of the sociological dimensions of "disability" (understood in the sense of impairment) and "disabling barriers" which affect people with impairments in quite different ways.

A confounding issue which arises whenever one discusses the experience of disability is that many people don't want to be identified as "disabled". In part, this may reflect the stigma of disability, in part it may reflect the way they interpret their unique embodiment. The visibility of a disability also affects people's identity choices as well - some people feel that they can hide their disabilities, whereas others experience obvious physical which are impossible to hide (for instance, a spinal cord injury which requires the use of a wheelchair). This means there are often differences in the lives of people who have visible disabilities (for instance, someone who uses a white cane, or who has a service dog) and those who do not have a visible disability (for instance, someone with a history of mental illness). And this difference can affect whether the people seek assistance from disability agencies, whether they seek (or receive) services or treatment, and how well they cope with their daily lives. It is a very complex experience, and both visible and invisible disabilities can cause significant distress.

In recent years, the disability movement in the US has promoted the idea that disabled people constitute a clear minority group, with a history of oppression, segregation and exclusion, and that this group of people now deserves full citizenship rights. This approach may also be associated with the ideas of 'disability pride' and 'disability culture'. While I don't disagree at all with the message about inclusion, I do question the notion of a unified disability identity which often underlies such an argument. Nearly all of the (seemingly) 'disabled' people I have interviewed (people whose experiences ranged from Brain Injury to Blindness to Deafness to Autism to Cancer to Intellectual Disability) – hundreds and hundreds of people – do not identify as 'disabled'. This is an incredibly important backdrop to any discussions of disability – most 'disabled' people will not identify themselves as such, will not access appropriate accommodations and services, and may struggle with unaccommodating systems as a result.

Furthermore, there are major differences between different groups of 'disabled people' – not just differences in the ways their bodies, minds or senses operate, but equally importantly, there are major demographic differences between different impairments. Without acknowledging these differences, the danger is that wider patterns of privilege and exclusion will be reproduced – patterns of inequality such as racism and sexism.

In this context, this book is one small effort to increase awareness about the diversity of factors involved in the experience of disability. It has been stimulated by a number of impulses, such as the efforts of many people to improve awareness of issues of inequality and injustice associated with disability. These issues range from the presence of a 'disability hierarchy' which marginalizes people with non-visible disabilities to wider forms of injustice such as racism and sexism that are present in both the cultural construction of disability and also in responses to disability in both policy and practice. Part of the impetus for the book was to demonstrate that issues of sex, gender, ethnicity, and socioeconomic status are not 'side issues' to the study of disability. They are actually quite central to the incidence of disability, and patterns of inequality associated with these diverse demographic factors must be considered in order to develop appropriate responses to the needs of particular groups of disabled people.

DIVERSITY

The Oxford English Dictionary defines "diversity" as being "widely varied". Some of the markers of community diversity include differences in age, race, ethnicity, gender, and socioeconomic status. All of these factors influence whether someone develops a disability, and they also influence how a person can deal with their disability, when and if they acquire it. Diversity is a term used in many debates about community change, workplace reform, and education. The political arguments for diversity are based on the idea that by recognizing and responding effectively to diversity, we may help promote a culture of inclusion, rather than exclusion. Also, it is suggested that societies that value diversity show that they can recognize and respect individual and group differences, understand and tolerate the views of others, and communicate openly. Recognizing diversity suggests the need for flexibility, because "one size doesn't fit all". However, diversity can be managed in a way which promotes innovative ideas, new experiences and positive reforms. A diverse community, or even a diverse workforce, can be a source of innovation and energy – and only when it is regarded as a threat, will such potential be thwarted.

Recognizing diversity also means that we need to be careful, and attentive, to the differences which exist among different groups, and within groups, so that we address everyone's needs. Such awareness not only increases the sensitivity of doctors, allied health professionals and policy makers – but it also changes the way we communicate, assess, develop appropriate responses, and assess our own practice wisdom.

CONNECTING DISABILITY AND DIVERSITY

What does this mean for the connection between disability and diversity? Well, of course, that depends on our definitions of both "disability" and "diversity". And so we see that disability and diversity both come to be dealing with the same issue – respect for difference.

DISABILITY AS A DIVERSE EXPERIENCE

Disability is a very diverse experience. It affects some people's minds, some people's senses, other people's bodies, and so on. Someone who is hard of hearing is likely to have very different life experiences from someone who is blind, or another person who has a developmental disability. And they all will have different life stories to another person who has a serious mental illness, or someone else who has end-stage cancer. Even among disabled people, there are huge differences. We need to be mindful of the diversity among disabled people as one of the starting points for understanding any particular disability.

And disability is also influenced by many demographic factors – factors such as race, ethnicity, gender, age, geographic location, and socioeconomic status. Disability can affect any person, at any time – but some people are more at risk than others of developing disabilities. Some disabilities are genetic, and occur at higher rates in some ethnic populations than others – for instance, Tay-Sachs disease is an often-fatal genetic disability far more prevalent among Ashkenazi Jews than other ethnic groups (Duster, 2003). Some disabilities are more common among Caucasians (for instance, osteoporosis) whereas others are more common among African Americans (Lau, 2001). For instance, Uterine Leiomyomata, commonly called Fibroids, are the leading cause of hysterectomy in the United States and occur far more frequently among African American women than among Caucasian women (Boynton-Jarrett, Rich-Edwards, Malspeis, Missmer, & Wright, 2005). These differences also apply to other ethnic groups - Native Americans experience much higher rates of Diabetes (Stansbury, Jia, Williams, Vogel, & Duncan, 2005), and Hawaiian/Pacific Islander people experience much higher rates of Obesity than other ethnic groups (Baruffi, Hardy, Waslien, Uyehara, & Krupitsky, 2004).

Some people imply that disability is an "equal opportunity experience" by suggesting that it could happen to anyone at any time, without recognizing that various groups face different risks of disability. For instance, Thomson states that because "anyone can become disabled at any time" (Thomson, 1997). What this argument ignores is that we live in a society where social inequalities, wars, violence, and so on directly and indirectly cause disability. This means that these forms of injustice get reproduced in the patterns of disability, such as gun-related head injuries or head injuries from domestic violence. African Americans and Hispanics are more likely than other ethnic groups to acquire disabilities as a result of gang-related violence and gunshots (Soriano, Rivera, Williams, Daley, & Reznik, 2004).

Language barriers, geography and cultural familiarity are also significant in creating inequalities. Cultural practices that differ from group to group may also contribute to the incidence of disability. Also, racism, bias and stereotyping can mean that people get a lower quality of service when they attend health care settings – for instance, African Americans, and in some cases, Hispanics, are less likely than whites to receive appropriate cardiac medication or to undergo coronary artery bypass surgery, less likely to get peritoneal dialysis and kidney transplants. Even when people have the same income and insurance level, racial and ethnic minorities receive lower quality health care, and this leads to disabilities – things like more amputations for patients with Diabetes. It also means that statistically, as patients, they have a higher mortality rate (Smedley, Stith, & Nelson, 2003).

Disability has an interesting relationship with geography, as well. Some disabilities are more likely to occur in particular climates. For instance, there is a clearly established relationship between Multiple Sclerosis and climate – meaning that people who live in particular sorts of climates have a greater risk of developing Multiple Sclerosis than others. Likewise, there are some climates which reduce the risk. In the USA, people who live in the Southern States have a much lower risk of developing Multiple Sclerosis, whereas people who live in the Northern States have a much higher rate (Kurtzke, Beebe, & Norman, 1979).

There are also some geographic areas where a particular disability is highly concentrated. For instance, historically, there was a very high rate of congenital Deafness in Martha's Vineyard – in fact, such a high level of deafness that virtually everyone at Martha's Vineyard knew Sign Language at one stage (Groce, 2006). The degree to which the local community accommodated the needs of deaf people further encouraged large numbers of deaf people to settle at Martha's Vineyard.

Other disabilities occur in specific areas because of patterns of social exclusion. For instance, Molokai, the fifth largest island in the Hawaiian archipelago, contains an area known as Kalaupapa where people diagnosed with Leprosy were historically segregated and exiled. The area of Kalaupapa was chosen for this leprosarium because it was relatively easy to isolate, being bordered by the Pacific Ocean on three sides, and 2000 feet cliffs on the fourth side. From 1866 until 1969, over 8000 people were forcibly removed from their communities and required to live in Kalaupapa. This constituted the longest example of medical segregation in US history. Today, leprosy is called Hansen's Disease (named after the Norwegian doctor who discovered the germ that causes the disease) and antibodies have been used to cure it since 1942. The terms "leper" and "leprosy" are now regarded as insulting slurs, loaded with stigma and mythology. The disease is not as highly contagious as once feared: only 5% of people have a genetic susceptibility to contacting it. As of 2006, there are still approximately 40 people on Kalaupapa and their average age is 75. This remains by far the highest concentration of people with Hansen's disease in the USA (Sherry, forthcoming-b).

Another factor which is important in terms of understanding the diversity of disability experiences, is that acquiring a disability at a young age is a completely different experience than gaining it as a natural part of the ageing process. The identity that a person develops, for instance, is completely different, the social barriers they experience are different, and the lifetime economic costs are totally different. For instance, someone who acquires a disability as a result of Cerebral Palsy (which happens in the first 4 months of life) will have very different experiences compared to someone who gets a head injury in their mid-twenties or another person who acquires Alzheimer's Disease later in life.

Age is also an important factor to consider in relation to disability. For example, more than 50% of all spinal cord injuries occur to people between the ages of 16 and 30 (Ditunno & Formal, 1994). Knowledge of the relationship between disability and age can profoundly impact on the way society understands a problem, and responds to it. (The implication of this particular statistic is that there may be a need to specifically target people from the ages of 16 to 30 from engaging in the sorts of risky behaviors that increase their chances of getting a spinal cord injury, such as drink driving or speeding).

Furthermore, some disabilities are more prevalent among women than men (for instance, Multiple Sclerosis), whereas other disabilities are more common among men than women (for instance, Deafness and Spinal Cord Injury). In emphasizing diversity, it begins apparent there are major differences between men and women with disabilities which need to be examined – issues which often get overlooked. For instance – when discussing the experiences of people with Epilepsy, it is rare for epilepsy organizations to address the issue of pregnancy. It is rare for doctors in the field (neurologists, who are mainly male) to concentrate on the effects of anti-seizure drugs on women with seizure disorders. And yet the chances of a baby with a disability are affected both by having seizures, and by taking anticonvulsants. Women with seizures have a somewhere between a 4 and 17% chance of having a baby with developmental disabilities such as Spina Bifida, Congenital Heart Disease, or Cleft Palate. The estimates vary, and there are huge debates over them. However, women without seizures have 1-2% chance. Also, fertility is generally reduced by 20% in women with Epilepsy, as a result of the combined effect of seizures and anti-seizure medications. Women on anti-seizure medications can breastfeed. Although the anti-convulsants are found in the breastmilk, they are in low (safe) amounts. So, it is clear that there is a desperate need to be aware of the diverse needs of people with Epilepsy (including issues specific to women with epilepsy) in order to address all their medical and social needs (Morrell & Flynn, 2003).

Even among women, there are major differences when it comes to disability experiences. For instance, Caucasian women are more likely to develop breast cancer than are women from any other ethnic group, but African American women have a much lower 5 year survival rate from breast cancer when they develop it (Blackman & Masi, 2006). It is important to pay attention to these sorts of differences so that policy and practical responses to disability are appropriate.

Attention to diversity is not a matter of political correctness – it can be a matter of life and death, as cases such as this demonstrate.

As well, some disabilities occur very differently in men and women. Cancer is an important cause of disability. But when we look at different types of cancers, the development of the cancers is greatly affected by gender. One obvious example is breast cancer, where the gender differences are well known. But many other forms of cancer, such as anal cancer, are less well known. The term "anal cancer" refers to any form of cancer associated with the anus. According to the National Cancer Institute, anal cancer is estimated to affect 4,660 people in the USA in 2006, and is expected to result in 660 deaths. There are many types of malignant and benign cancers, as well as precancerous conditions, which can be found in the anal canal (a canal approximately an inch and a half long, connected to the rectum). Anal cancer affects men and women differently. Men tend to get anal cancer outside the anus, whereas women tend to get anal cancer inside the anus. Although most forms of anal cancer can be cured, women experience a mortality rate from anal cancer which is approximately twice the rate experienced by men. Importantly, from a diversity perspective, one recent study also suggests that black men have a higher rate of anal cancer, and lower survival rates, than other race-specific and gender-specific groups (Sherry, forthcoming-a).

A SOCIOLOGICAL PERSPECTIVE

While this book engages with debates from public health, epidemiology, disability studies and other disciplines, its intention is to analyze disability from a sociological perspective – that is, to focus on the multiple issues of power which influence the creation of disabilities and the presence of disabling barriers. This sociological focus means that the book does not simply analyze any disability as simply a physical/mental condition – disability is always experienced in contexts that are racialized, gendered, classed, ethicized, aged, and so on. Highlighting these aspects of power as they influence people's everyday lives distinguishes a sociological perspective from these other perspectives.

Whereas an epidemiological perspective might stop knowing that multiple sclerosis is far more common among women than men, a sociological perspective requires more analysis. It requires us to ask – what does this mean in terms of policy responses? How is the gendered nature of this disability incorporated (or not) into the policies and practices of disability agencies, service providers, and policy makers? Are there specific gender issues (for instance, around pregnancy or around domestic violence) which need to be addressed once this disability is understood in its social context?

And in terms of those disabilities, such as diabetes, which occur more commonly in ethnic/racial groups such as Native Americans, a sociological approach demands that responses to this disability are critically examined in order to see if they are culturally relevant, inclusive, and nondiscriminatory. Indeed, a sociological approach may identify particular disabling barriers which exist because such responses are culturally inappropriate.

DISABILITY, ILLNESS, DISEASE, DISORDER?

One of the most difficult, and interesting, aspects of this book is the way certain conditions are labeled "disabilities", whereas others are considered "disorders", "illnesses" or "diseases". The diverse terms that can be used to describe any medical condition mean that definitions of such terms are often very complex, contested, and even overlapping. The definition of disability, while seemingly uncomplicated, is actually one of most difficult and controversial topics in disability studies (and to a lesser degree, public health and sociology). Historically, medical sociology has addressed this question (somewhat) through use of the concept of the 'sick role', developed by Talcott Parsons in the 1950s. Parsons' approach was innovative because it stressed that sickness was a social role, as much as a medical condition. He believed that being sick provided both rights and obligations – absolving them from responsibility for their condition and exempting them from their regular social roles, alongside the obligation to work with medical professionals to try to get better. There are, however, many flaws with Tarson's approach – which are well known in sociological theory (Sherry, 2006). Such flaws include the assumption that sickness is a temporary role, rather than a permanent one, and that the underlying assumption that relationships with health professionals are characterized by consensus rather than conflict.

In disability studies, the 'sick role' concept is largely ignored, and the focus has turned from illness to a broader concept of 'disability' (Oliver, 1990). This does not entirely solve the problem, however, because there are a number of different ways to define 'disability'. One of the most popular is known as "the social model of disability". The social model separates 'impairment' (a physical or mental condition) from 'disability' (understood as negative social reactions or prejudice towards people with those impairments) (Sherry, 2006). This approach is particularly important in Britain, where disabled people's organizations have struggled to influence policy and practice by politicizing the presence of disabling barriers (Priestley, 1999). The social model has also been raised at international disability conferences, and has supporters in Australia, New Zealand, the United States, Canada, and many other countries. The strength of the social model is that it suggests the 'problem' is not with the bodies or minds of disabled people, the problem is that society does not accommodate everyone. However, by (largely) ignoring the issue of impairment, this model has left itself open to the criticism that it takes an asocial approach to illness or disease – precisely the problem that Parsons was seeking to rectify over 50 years ago.

An alternative approach to disability, stemming predominantly from the United States (but also having adherents in many other countries) is to approach disability as an identity, and to regard people with disabilities as a minority group (Linton, 1998). (Unlike the social group model, which prefers the term 'disabled people', this approach uses the term 'people with disabilities'). This approach to disability is deeply rooted in identity politics, and promotes the idea that disabled people are a minority with unique experiences and knowledge that others do not share (Siebers, 2006). The problem with this approach, of course, it that presents a binary – supposedly there are one group of people who have such unique (embodied and social) knowledge, and another who do not. Whether someone who has a particular illness, or a certain disease, fits this definition of 'disability' is a matter of contestation and political wrangling. The debate over who is 'really disabled' – who has an 'authentic' disability identity – is often a matter of intense scrutiny and exclusion. Furthermore, claims that disability involves unique forms of embodied knowledge seem quite spurious, given that the definition of disability in such identity politics is so unstable and open to contestation.

Rather than seeking to 'solve' this contradiction, the purpose of this book is to explore it, to indulge it, and to promote questioning as opposed to simple answers. The exact point when a 'disease' becomes a disability for an individual cannot be known in advance; likewise, the importance of a particular 'disorder' may vary from one person to the next, or one situation to the next. Some people may choose to adopt a disability identity in some contexts but not in others. This inconsistently cannot be resolved, or explained away – it is a fundamental part of identity. Attempts to 'shore up' or consolidate disability as a fixed identity, rather than to explore all of its nuances, subtleties and contradictions are overly simplistic in this context.

One of the reasons for the complication, and expansion, of the term disability – including its blurring with various forms of illness, disease and other disorders – may be what Conrad calls "the medicalization of society" (Conrad, 2007). Conrad believes that there is an increasing tendency to label "normal human conditions" (ranging from various behavior issues to menopause and even sexual dysfunction) as medical issues – with an associated expansion of the medical domain and significant implications for our concepts of health and illness. Likewise, he argues that the public has become less tolerant of mild symptoms over time and have engaged in "diagnostic advocacy" to raise public awareness of life with particularly misunderstood conditions. The case of Multiple Chemical Sensitivity is an example where such advocacy has been extensively carried out; at once demonstrating how such activism is both a consequence and catalyst for changed understanding of the condition.

Conrad does not attribute 'blame' to doctors for the process of medicalization; that would be too simplistic. Instead, his work frames medicalization as a social process which is much more expansive than direct medical care or diagnosis – the expansion of medical categories into collective social understandings of common life processes. One implication of this process is that definitions of concepts such as 'health', 'illness', 'disease', 'disorder' and 'disability' may be far more fluid than previously assumed. Conrad stresses that this fluid social process is bidirectional – while the overall trend has been to medicalize various conditions, there have been numerous cases of demedicalization also. Conrad suggests that a classic example of demedicalization (historically speaking) was the demedicalization of masturbation.

There is, however, another (perhaps more dangerous) aspect to the debate over definitions of disability. Some prominent disability advocates have been unconsciously relying on a very restrictive notion of 'disability' which specifically excludes those with infectious diseases. For instance, one very well known early Canadian disability studies book was entitled "Disability is not Measles" - with the theme that one cannot 'catch' disability (Rioux & Bach, 1994). This is of course a mistaken argument – one can 'catch' AIDS, one can acquire leprosy contagiously, and so on. And one can certainly experience the spread of stigma as a result of developing various physical, sensory, cognitive or psychological conditions.

Moreover, there is a danger that the ways in which we understand disability (including the social experiences associated with it) may reflect the power of those who have advocated loudest about it, but not those who are particularly marginalized even though they share some common experiences. For instance, it is well known that the people who began the first Centers for Independent Living in the US were wheelchair users (Shapiro, 1994). Some authors have subsequently criticized the marginalization of people with non-physical disabilities in such organizations, labeling this process the creation of a "disability hierarchy" (Deal, 2003). But what such discussions have not raised is an equally important point from the perspective of diversity: whether the organizations established by (and advocating for) the rights of wheelchair users – such as Centers for Independent Living – have even advocated for all of the people who use wheelchairs. Given that African Americans are more likely to receive spinal cord injuries through gang violence than Caucasians, it might be reasonable to suggest that the failure of Centers for Independent Living to address issues associated with gangs, drug cultures, and violence simply reflects their historical neglect of key issues for people of color. Likewise, the failure of Centers for Independent Living to prioritize issues of abuse – even though some surveys of disabled women have placed this issue at the top of their priorities – again raises the issue of whether such organizations are only representing a privileged section of the disability community.

Identifying the diversity of people with disabilities, disorders, diseases and illnesses is therefore an important political, personal and practical issue. Knowing that a particular condition is more likely to be experienced by women than men, or by African American people rather than Hispanics, is important because it helps to identify those groups whose needs are being met – as well as those whose needs are being unmet. It is therefore an important issue in terms of both equity and efficiency.

There is one more important point to be made in this discussion. The most complex (and for me, the most interesting) issues associated with discussions of 'disability' involve the naming question: who names who, what the name is, and what to do about it. In general, I prefer to use the term 'disabled people' as opposed to 'people with disabilities'. I generally do not use 'people-first language' because I want to emphasize the political nature of choices made by people around identity. I also bristle against any sense of identity intolerance which implies only one phrase is suitable for a widely varied population. Sometimes I throw in the term 'people with disabilities' just to further unsettle expectations.

I completely understand the arguments on both sides of this debate, but I now choose to side with neither (at least not permanently!). I understand why some people want to distance 'the person' from 'the disability' – even though that sounds a rather disembodied conception of identity to me. I understand the argument that it is important to acknowledge the multi-dimensional lives of people, and not simply the physical, sensory, psychological or other aspects of their lives which have been marked as 'abnormal' in some setting. There is a similar argument, in fact, made by those who prefer the term 'disabled people' to the more common 'people with disabilities'. The term 'disabled people' is used to emphasize that the person's embodiment is quite different from their experiences of 'disability' – a term which is used to refer to barriers that limit the rights, freedoms and opportunities of people with various impairments. Again – while I appreciate this emphasis on what I would like to call 'disabling barriers' – I am not convinced about the disembodied discussion of disabling barriers. So… I generally use the term "disabled people" as a political effort to emphasize the importance of disabling barriers – but I sometimes use the term "people with disabilities", simply to demonstrate that I am in some ways uneasy with the former term.

ADDRESSING DISABLING BARRIERS

It is tempting, especially when one considers epidemiological data, to focus more on the unequal social division of illnesses/disabilities/disorders/medical conditions without acknowledging the similarities (and indeed, differences) in experience of disabling barriers. The term "disabling barriers", in this context, designates those physical and attitudinal barriers which prevent disabled people from fully participating in the community.

Some disability activists suggest that the one thing common to all disabled people is that they have experienced some form of disabling barrier. Oliver for example comments:

> All disabled people experience disability as social restriction whether these restrictions occur as a consequence of inaccessible built environments, questionable notions of intelligence and social competence, the inability of the general public to use sign language, the lack of material in Braille or hostile public attitudes to people with non-visible disabilities (Oliver, 1990: .xiv).

Oliver's comments are useful in one respect: they begin to suggest that disabling barriers take many shapes and forms. Disabling barriers may be physical (such as buildings without ramps or other forms of physical access), social (such as the use of jargon and confusing language/terminology around people with particular cognitive impairments), visual/audio-based (such as the failure to provide Braille, speech-to-text, or other assisted communication devices for blind and vision impaired people), communication-based (such as the failure to provide Sign Language interpreters for Deaf and hard of hearing people), environmental (such as the failure to address inappropriate lighting for people with Epilepsy and Seizure disorders, or the failure to remove certain toxic chemicals for people with Multiple Chemical Sensitivity), financial (such as those cost barriers which prevent some poorer disabled people from obtaining necessary treatments or drugs) or attitudinal (such as prejudice against people with mental illness or ignorance about other less-common disabilities). Disabling barriers may also be a combination of any of these factors, or may even take additional forms.

Disabling barriers have such terrible consequences effects on people's lives (limiting their rights, freedoms, hopes and opportunities) that they have been framed as a form of 'institutional discrimination' (Swain, Gillman, & French, 1998). Prejudices are enacted in various negative attitudes (cognitive, emotional and behavioral); environments can be inflexible because of disablist language, institutional policies, professional practices, or inaccessible physical environments; and structural inequalities and barriers can disempower disabled people and deny them human rights (Swain et al., 1998). But it is too simplistic to imply a commonality across all disability groups, in the way that Oliver has done - and to a lesser extent, Swain, Gilman and French - without acknowledging that particular groups experience unique barriers, some more or less than others, and that there is a complex (rather than simple) relationship between the nature of the impairment and the experience of particular disabling barriers.

To recognize that disability is a *particular form* of social oppression, which is clearly Oliver's intention, requires that a specific connection be made between particular forms of embodiment, sensation, or cognition, and particular social/discursive reactions to those body forms. Different forms of disability cannot be automatically assumed to have similar experiences of disabling barriers, without a-priori investigation. For instance, one cannot assume that the experience of disabling barriers which may accompany one particular form of vision loss (let's say, for example, Stargardt's Disease) will be the same for other forms of vision loss, even ones with similar symptoms such as Age-Related Macular Generation, which typically affect a much older population. And it is a huge stretch of the imagination to assume that someone with a completely different disability, such as Multiple Personality Disorder, or someone with an autoimmune condition such as Celiac Disease (with symptoms of chronic diarrhea, fatigue, weight loss and stunted growth in children) would have similar experiences of social, physical, communication, sensory, visual or audio-based barriers.

The journal *Disability and Society* contains many practical applications of the social model of disability to particular disabilities. Recent editions have covered Celiac Disease (Carrie & Chan, 2008), Multiple Chemical Sensitivity (Gibson & Lindberg, 2007), and Vision Impairment (Percival, Hanson, & Osipovic, 2006). According to Percival, Hanson and Osipovic, for instance, people with vision impairments have unique needs associated with domestic and outside space, home location, safety and security.

The purpose of this discussion is not to suggest that there are no commonalities between people with different disabilities. Disabled people may feel particular affinities with each other, based on life shared experiences, but a sense of commonality must be discursively constructed – and this usually occurs through particular forms of identity politics. That is, people construct a group identity and engage in pressure group activities or form a social movement based on their perceived common interests. In this political process, however, there are no guarantees of inclusion. And there are multiple traps and pitfalls that can lead to exclusion. All of these political factors can contribute to different disabling barriers.

A fascinating exploration of some of the ways in which discourse is central to the construction (and contestation) of disability identity has been conducted by Nancy Bagatell who examined the process of identity construction for one Autistic boy (Bagatell, 2007). Her choice of an autistic person as a focus for investigating wider social processes about identity construction is particularly interesting because people who are autistic are commonly assumed to be less responsive to the social environment (and presumably less sensitive to social pressures about their own identities). Indeed, the difficulties people with autism experience in social interactions and communication has led many authors to assert that autistic people struggle to establish a sense of self. On the other hand, Bagatell's research with one 21 year old man with Asperger's Syndrome indicated that this man was remarkably creative in the ways he defined his own self and struggled with social expectations about (not) being 'normal'. Bagatell records his attempts to build an alternative sense of self (without ignoring the frustrations, disappointments and even suicidal ideation which he experienced) – pointing towards the broader issue, for many disabled people, of trying to challenge and re-define negative identities associated with particular disabilities.

CONCLUSION

This chapter has provided an outline of the terms disability and diversity. Recognizing diversity is important – it is important to be very conscious of the fact that groups of disabled people have vastly different experiences, so that appropriate responses are developed. People with different disabilities have very different lives and identities, and even people with the same disability can have very different experiences because of their gender, race, ethnicity, socioeconomic status, age or because of a range of other factors. In order to respond effectively to the diverse needs of disabled people, it is essential to be conscious of their multiple identities – as men or women, as members of ethnic groups, as young or older people, and so on. By highlighting diversity within disability experiences, it becomes apparent that even people with the same disability have very different experiences because of the place they live, the work they do, the ethnic group they belong to, and so on. It is an issue that is so much more complex than many people assume.

Chapter 2

DISABILITY AND ETHNICITY

This chapter will examine the connections between disability and ethnicity. As indicated in Chapter One, particular ethnic groups face higher risks of certain disabilities and health conditions. The chapter will highlight the unequal ethnic distribution of many disabilities, including Multiple Sclerosis, Heart Disease, Cystic Fibrosis, Migraine, and Mental Illness. One of the primary sources of information about the unequal ethnic distribution of mental illness which will be considered in this chapter is Surgeon General's report on ethnic and racial disparities in mental health, which will be discussed in some detail.

DEFINING ETHNICITY

When people discuss the idea of an "ethnic group", they usually mean a group which is unified by a common culture. In this way, ethnicity can refer to a shared history, language, family structure, religion or occupation, etc. Ethnicity is not assumed to imply common biological traits, but instead a shared social history. The term 'race' is often considered anachronistic within sociological literature because of its pejorative and racist undertones, as well as its lack of scientific grounding. As a result, the term race is often placed in quotation marks – as in discussions of 'race' – to highlight its problematic nature. Also, for this reason, the use of the concept of 'ethnicity' it usually regarded as less problematic than the idea of 'race' (Karner, 2007). Nevertheless, a great deal of the literature on epidemiology tends to use 'racial' categories – and this chapter will rely on these categories in some instances, simply to report their findings, even though the 'racial' terms which are employed are often problematic. Sometimes, the use of 'racial' categories is purposeful – it is designed to explore possible genetic or biological components of disabilities – but often it is simply a sloppy, shorthand attempt to identify ethnic differences.

Nevertheless, it should not be assumed that 'ethnicity' is a term without complexities and contradictions. Sociological studies of ethnicity have found that ethnic identification is far more fluid than it may at first appear. In terms of sociological analyses of ethnicity, Mary Waters' study of ethnic identity among 'white' Americans quickly became a landmark study in the critical analysis of "whiteness" (Waters, 1990). What was most interesting about her research was that she found a remarkable degree of *flux* and *choice* about ethnic identities. The key finding of this research was that later-generation ethnicity is dynamic and involves choices. The complexity of the mechanisms which people used in their ethnic identities ethnicities was fascinating: ethnic identification was not an automatic process, it shifted and changed over the life course and was subject to both choice and constraint.

Waters also demonstrated that ethnicity was often subject to simplification and distortion. People in her study often sifted or sorted through their identities so that their "hidden ancestries" did not arise until extensive probing by the researcher. Acknowledging ethnic identities also changed across the life course: between the ages of 15 and 24, young adults often simplified their ancestries by identifying primarily with one or two ethnic identities (and not others). Additionally, between 30 and 60 percent of children were not labeled as the exact combination of their parents' ancestries – highlighting the changing intergenerational nature of ethnicity. Many of these children had new and different identities from their parents – in some cases, this involved the ascription of an "American" identity, though this choice was heavily influenced by parental country of origin and was by no means automatic. Likewise, although there was often a preference for choosing the father's ancestry in the process of ethnic identification, this was also not uniform across different European ancestries. Some paternal ancestries were likely to be claimed far more often than others (for instance, it was far more likely for a person whose father was Italian to choose that identity than someone whose father was Scottish). Marriage also influenced ethnic identification: unmarried women were more likely to report mixed ancestry than married women (highlighting the fact that ethnicity is a mixture of social and individual factors).

As well, socioeconomic status greatly affected the recognition of certain ethnicities. People with a higher socioeconomic status were more likely to have some knowledge about their grandparents' ethnic backgrounds whereas people who were poorer were more likely to lack this knowledge and regard themselves as what Waters calls "unhyphenated whites". Waters' emphasis on the changing nature of ethnicity – both over the life course, and according to the nature of an individual's personal relationships and class status – was an important breakthrough in sociological theorizing of this concept and must be remembered when analyzing data on ethnicity, health and disability.

Waters' research suggested that the choice of ethnicity for Caucasians was influenced by many social factors. These factors included marital status, socioeconomic status, age, ethnicity (with some ethnicities more likely to be claimed than others), experiences of discrimination and perceptions of cultural stereotypes, and so on. However, it should not be assumed that ethnicity is plastic only for 'unhyphenated whites'. Miri Song's research on the experiences of ethnic minorities in the US and the UK came to similar conclusions (Song, 2003). The theme of Song's work is that within certain constraints, members of ethnic minorities are also able to exercise ethnic options, and move in directions towards their desired ethnic identities.

Song begins by acknowledging that we can make choices – for instance, choosing "Asian American" as opposed to "Asian" or "American", but the *range* of ethnic options available to a person/group is not entirely under their control. Even then, if a person adopts a particular identity, there is no guarantee that others will apply it to them. Song suggests that by using stories, symbols and rituals in particular ways, and also by developing new forms of inter-group comparison, members of ethnic minorities can strategically shape their own identities. As well, Song discusses members of ethnic groups playing with various identities via masquerade and using such performances to manipulate the meanings of particular ethnic identities. Studies of ethnicity should not simply focus on lineage and ancestry, Song argues; it is equally important to examine the ways conceptions of ethnic identities are continually in flux.

DISABILITY AND ETHNIC DIVERSITY

Having outlined the complex and fluid nature of the concept of ethnicity, this section of the Chapter will nevertheless highlight the extraordinary diversity which can be found among various 'ethnic' groups in terms of many disabilities. The first disability to be discussed is Multiple Sclerosis (MS). MS is a disability which affects the central nervous system. It involves a breakdown of the myelin sheath (covering) which surrounds the brain, spinal cord and optic nerves. Scar tissue, or sclerosis, is left when this myelin sheath breaks down. MS frequently results in a loss of mobility, as well as producing cognitive and sensory changes.

There is a great degree of difference in the prevalence of MS according to ethnicity. Unfortunately, the literature on MS tends to use racial language, rather than identifying groups by ethnicity. Regardless, this literature clearly demonstrates that MS is far more common among Caucasians than other ethnic groups, and while African Americans do not experience as high rates as Caucasians, they do have a significantly higher rate than other racial/ethnic groups.

Another interesting aspect of MS is that those African Americans who do experience it tend to have a higher level of disability than their Caucasian counterparts. One of the differences between African Americans and Caucasians, for instance, is that African Americans require ambulatory assistance at an earlier age than Caucasians (Rinker, Trinkaus, Naismith, & Cross, 2007). This difference may be the result of the more rapid progression of MS among African Americans, and the higher level of cerebellar dysfunction which they experience (Naismith, Trinkaus, & Cross, 2006). What these statistics may suggest is that an organization serving people with MS, or an agency providing funding to such organizations, may be unconsciously biased (in terms of ethnicity) if it is not aware of the unique needs of African American people in this regard. Conversely, by understanding this data, an agency may be able to tailor services in a more appropriate manner and may therefore avoid any unintended bias in service delivery.

The case of Migraine is another disability which is worthy of attention. Migraine is interesting, as a disability, because it reminds us that disability can be short-term as well as permanent. In the case of Migraine, like that of MS, there are not only differences in the actual rates of a disability among different ethnic groups, but also different degrees of severity (Stewart, Lipton, & Liberman, 1996). It appears that the incidence of Migraine is not only lower among African Americans than other ethnic groups, but the overall effects of Migraine reported by African Americans seemed to be less disabling than those reported by Asian Americans and Caucasians.

Stewart, Lipton and Liberman's survey of over 12,000 people in Baltimore, Maryland, suggests that among African Americans and Asian Americans, there are much lower rates of Migraines compared to Migraines in Caucasians. The exact results of the study indicate that 20.4% of Caucasian women reported Migraines, compared to 16.2% of African American women and 9.2% of Asian women. This study was also important in terms of highlighting the ways in which gender also affects the risks faced by members of different ethnic groups. Men consistently report lower levels of Migraine than do women. Among Caucasian men, 8.7% reported Migraines, compared to 7.2% of African American men and

4.2% of Asian American men. Another of the interesting findings of this study was that although there were higher rates of headache pain reported by African Americans than among Caucasians and Asian Americans, they also reported lower rates of nausea and vomiting (Stewart et al., 1996).

While this data on racial/ethnic variations in Migraine rates itself is quite interesting, it is equally important to examine the differences in responding to such experiences. This is where it becomes apparent that different ethnicities experience quite distinct barriers. An interesting example of such disparities involves the use of opiods to treat people with Migraines. A national sample of emergency department placements indicated that among people with complaints that were regarded as somewhat subjective (such as Migraine and back pain), the dispensation of analgesics did not appear to indicate any ethnic bias, but the dispensation of stronger drugs, such as opiods, certainly did. This study indicated that African Americans were far less likely to be dispensed opiods than members of other ethnicities (Tamayo-Sarver, Hinze, Cydulka, & Baker, 2003)

The unequal treatment of minority ethnic groups in the healthcare system has been the focus of a great deal of attention over many years. A recent literature review of studies about pain and pain medication seems to suggest that African Americans and Hispanics are less likely to have their pain documented on the medical record, are more likely to have their pain untreated, and are less likely than Caucasians to receive opiod analgesics for pain (Cintron & Morrison, 2006). However, this literature review did not suggest that patterns of unequal treatment were universal. For some conditions, it suggested that racial and ethnic disparities appeared to be absent. For instance, it reported a review of the treatment of patients with long-bone fractures in emergency departments which did not find any patterns of racial or ethnic disparities. Such reports suggest that medical practice can (and does) provide nondiscriminatory healthcare in certain areas; criticisms of disparities should be targeted only where appropriate.

It is (of course) inadequate to simply recognize that these disparities exist without analyzing the issues further and making recommendations to improve the situation. One of the implications here is that healthcare professionals and organizations require retraining and many policies and practices need to be reformed. But that is only part of the solution. Organizations which represent and advocate for people with particular conditions like Migraine (such as the National Migraine Association, the American Council for Headache Education, the American Headache Society) must also place greater emphasis on education and advocacy about such disparities.

Heart disease is another disability where there are marked differences among different ethnicities. A range of risk factors for cardiovascular disease, including obesity, hypertension, and physical inactivity are unevenly distributed among the population. The incidence of Heart Disease and Stroke is higher among African Americans than Caucasians – and is also higher among men than women (Mensah, Mokdad, Ford, Greenlund, & Croft, 2005). Not only does the incidence of cardiovascular disease differ markedly among ethnic groups, the quality of treatment which different ethnic groups receive is also quite disparate. One study of almost 28,000 people in New York who had experienced Coronary Artery Bypass surgery indicated that the surgeons who operated on African Americans and Asians/Pacific Islanders tended to have less successful surgical records than surgeons who operated on other ethnic/racial groups. It was estimated that operations provided by these less-successful surgeons led to an additional 170 minority deaths across the US nationally (Rothenberg, Pearson, Zwanziger, & Mukamel, 2004).

Inherent in these differences in heart disease are significant gender differences. Sociologically, this is an important issue, because it suggests that disabilities are not only differently racialized or ethnicized, they are always sexed as well. The need to understand these multiple identities suggests that it is necessary to adopt a perspective of "intersectionality" in order to understand the interaction of multiple sites of power (and marginalization) on a person's overall health status. An example of the value of such an approach can be found in the experiences of men and women who have a heart attack, coronary heart disease or congestive heart failure in association with other illnesses such diabetes, hypertension and end-stage renal disease. Men and women have markedly different mortality rates from coronary heart disease – the reported mortality rate for African American men is 250.6 per 100,000, compared to 220.5 for White men, 169.7 for African American women, and 131.2 for Caucasian women (Correa-de-Araujo et al., 2006).

Coronary heart disease has a quite different epidemiological distribution than heart attacks. The average age of women having a heart attack is 76, compared to an average age of 64 for men and the mortality rate for women within one year of the heart attack is significantly higher than the mortality rate for men. (Correa-de-Araujo et al., 2006). But treatment of these conditions is also markedly different. In terms of the drugs dispensed to these patients, Caucasian men receive the highest rate of asprin, β-blockers and ACE inhibitors, followed by Caucasian women, with African American and Hispanic people of both sexes receiving these medications far less frequently. Likewise, Caucasians of both genders were more likely to receive smoking cessation education (Correa-de-Araujo et al., 2006).

There is a desperate need to address these disparities with a range of appropriate policy and practice interventions. Such interventions are required of health care professionals, policy experts and also relevant disability organizations.

The incidence of Ischemic Stroke for people with diabetes also demonstrates significant differences between African Americans and other ethnic groups. African Americans with diabetes typically experience Ischemic Strokes ten years earlier than Caucasians with diabetes (Kissela et al., 2005). Public health interventions aimed at people with diabetes must recognize this diversity, so that targeted interventions can be developed which address these different epidemiological characteristics. Unless such differences in the risk factors for Stroke among people with diabetes are recognized, unconscious bias may result in an exacerbation of these health disparities. Again, there is an onus on both healthcare providers to reform their practices in this area as well as on disability advocacy organizations to educate and advocate on behalf of people who are disadvantaged by such disparities. Unfortunately, however, when one examines the publications and websites of disability organizations, one rarely sees any work on healthcare disparities. However, there are some organizations which have risen to this challenge. For instance, the American Heart Association has a section of its website dedicated to "Advocacy" which contains a section entitled "Learn Our Legislative and Regulatory Issues". In this section, it specifically raises the issue of healthcare disparities for minorities and also women. This sort of educational effort could be fairly easily incorporated into the websites of many other disability/illness advocacy organizations.

Another disability with marked differences in social distribution is Cystic Fibrosis. Cystic Fibrosis is a life-threatening disability which causes severe lung damage and digestive problems. It affects the cells in the body which produce mucus, sweat, saliva and digestive juices. While these secretions are normally thin and slippery, in cases of Cystic Fibrosis they become thick and sticky. The lungs and the pancreas are commonly affected, being clogged by the thick mucus. Also, key vitamins cannot be absorbed in the body due to the mucus clogging the pancreas.

In terms of a focus on diversity, it is fascinating to see that while the greatest single risk factor for developing Cystic Fibrosis is a family history of the disease, ethnicity is also hugely significant. There are much higher rates of Cystic Fibrosis among Caucasians than other ethnicities. Cystic Fibrosis is considered one of the most common lethal genetic diseases among Caucasians. However, the incidence of Cystic Fibrosis among other ethnic groups is much lower. A multi-center study of over 18,000 patients with Cystic Fibrosis in Northern America (i.e. over 60% of all people who have been diagnosed with Cystic Fibrosis) estimated that approximately 93% of reported cases involved Caucasians, 4% involved Hispanics, and 3% involved African Americans (Morgan et al., 1999). While this data is undoubtedly useful, a sociological perspective suggests that it is often important to deconstruct racial categories such as "Caucasian" in order to find ethnic differences and patterns of inconsistency.

The danger with using such all-embracing racial categories as "Caucasian" is that it may ignore significant ethnic differences among people within this category. For instance, in one study of Cystic Fibrosis among various groups of Jewish people, extreme differences were found. Indeed, the incidence of Cystic Fibrosis ranged from 1 in 2,400 to 1 in 39,000 in various Jewish groups (Kerem, 1997). The implication of this data is that specific targeted interventions may be more effective in turns of dealing with particular "Caucasian" groups, such as Jewish people. (Indeed, the changing racial status of Jewish people is itself a fascinating reflection of the interaction of power, racism, Anti-Semitism, and identity; the issue of whether Jews 'are really White' has a long history of contestation, ambivalence and denial). The implication of this data is that specific targeted interventions may be more effective in terms of dealing with particular "Caucasian" groups, such as Jewish people. This is fascinating, because one of the important components of Anti-Semitism, historically, has been an association of Jewish people with illness and disease (Gilman, 1985). And yet when there are real differences between the health status of Jewish people and others (such as in the case of Cystic Fibrosis), there are few existing public health strategies to specifically deal with this problem. Appropriate responses to this problem may include outreach aimed specifically at the Jewish community – but such interventions unfortunately do not seem to be on the radar of public health authorities or disability organizations.

As indicated in Chapter One, there are very important ethnic differences in the incidence of different types of cancer. For example, studies have consistently demonstrated that Vietnamese women experience much higher rates of cervical cancer than other ethnic groups. Cervical cancer is a serious issue which can lead to a loss of fertility, or even death. In the US, the rate of cervical cancer among Vietnamese women is estimated to be five times greater than those of Caucasians (Mock et al., 2007). Moreover, Asian Americans are particularly at risk of cancers which stem from an infectious origin and are the only ethnic group in the US for whom cancer is the leading cause of death (Chen, 2005). Once again, a sociological perspective is important in examining power differentials that may influence the equity of public health responses. This is not simply recognition of the need for culturally appropriate services – it involves an awareness of those forms of social inequality (such as racism, classism and sexism) which might make Vietnamese women a vulnerable group. A sociological perspective also highlights the overlap of economic, social and cultural barriers which influence the vulnerability of certain groups through every stage of the process of living with cancer, from prevention, detection and diagnosis to treatment, post-treatment quality of life, and survival and mortality (Ward et al., 2004)

Typically, many people do not consider cancer as a form of disability. And even more than that, they tend to assume that anything to do with sexual organs is a 'private' or 'personal' matter. Of course this is a problematic assumption – feminists have long argued that 'the personal is political'. Signs and symptoms of advanced cervical cancer can include back and leg pain, weight loss and fatigue, vaginal bleeding and leaking of urine or feces from the vagina, and bone fractures. Of course, when one considers these symptoms, one begins to realize that this is a serious disability indeed.

Unfortunately, despite the fact that Vietnamese women experience the highest risks for cervical cancer, and Asian people in general experience the highest death rates from cancer, there has often been a failure by relevant disability organizations to provide even the most basic information about these health disparities. It would be too simple to say that the relevant organizations should just put some of this information about health disparities on their websites, provide information in a culturally appropriate manner, and provide information in various languages other than English. (Having said that, neither the American Cancer Society's website nor the National Cervical Cancer Coalition has any information in languages other than English or Spanish). What is needed is a far broader awareness of diversity within the particular disability/illness/condition from people running these organizations and advocating on these issues. In a sense, these organizations could be leading the charge to remove halth disparities discrepancies – but they often appear unaware that such discrepancies even exist.

The issue of reproductive health also highlights the effects of 'race', class and gender on health and illness. Women bear the majority of the effects of reproductive choices and the majority of reproductive diseases. These diseases are also unevenly distributed (by income, for instance, where poor women have twice the rate of unintended pregnancies than the national average). Likewise, African American women have Fibroids at twice or three times the rate of Caucasian women. Sexually transmitted diseases are also unevenly distributed. In 1998, African American women reported Gonorrhea at 27 times higher than Caucasians, and Congenital Syphilis is reported 30 times higher among African American women than Caucasian women, and 9 times greater among Hispanics than Caucasians. Some of the measures proposed to reduce these disparities include: programs specifically aimed at reducing the risk of unwanted pregnancies;

programs to delay sexual activity among young people; research on the reasons for the under-utilization of infertility services by minority populations; and research on ways to improve prevention, screening and treatment of sexually transmitted diseases (Development, 2000).

There are a range of social factors which influence the incidence of certain diseases, illnesses and disabilities. One of the historical effects of racism in the US, for instance, is the concentration of African American people in certain ethnic enclaves; this historical pattern of residential segregation has ongoing effects on health and illness within these communities. Neighborhoods not only differ in terms of the recreational facilities they offer or their perceived safety, they also impact on the mental health of the people who live there. However, estimating the exact magnitude of 'neighborhood effects' is difficult because it raises many methodological, practical and theoretical complexities (Diez Roux, 2004). Nevertheless, the common-sense notion that neighborhood affluence, (or neighborhood poverty) does impact on the health and welfare of its members is widely accepted (Williams & Jackson, 2005). Many studies indicate that social disadvantage at the community or neighborhood level influences all aspects of health, including mental health, from the cradle to the grave. For instance, children in poor neighborhoods tend to have higher rates of mental illness than do their counterparts in more affluent areas, even accounting for other factors such as family demographics and maternal depression (Xue, Leventhal, Brooks-Gunn, & Earls, 2005)

Such statistics are sometimes regarded as problematic. There may be reluctance to associate higher rates of mental illness with particular ethnic groups, because of the fear that racism, combined with the stigma of mental illness, may lead to higher rates of discrimination or prejudice. Nevertheless, many reports have reported higher rates of various forms of mental illness among certain racial/ethnic groups. (Members of these ethnic groups often experience lower socioeconomic status – itself a strong risk factor for mental illness – and it is therefore prudent to assume that these figures reflect the complex interaction of culturally-specific and economic factors). Various explanations of this phenomenon have been offered:

- Members of certain ethnic minorities experience higher level of allopathic stress (associated with discrimination, prejudice, lower socioeconomic status, living in places with more environmental problems, and so forth) which lead to higher levels of mental illness;
- The higher levels of reported mental illness actually reflect bias among clinicians and healthcare professionals who mislabel 'mental

illness' among members of ethnic minorities because they misunderstand certain cultural norms or behaviors;

- Disparities in services available for ethnic minorities, rather than differences in the prevalence of mental illness, lead to higher rates of reported mental illness; and/or
- Some ethnic groups have a higher genetic predisposition to certain illnesses or disabilities.

The Surgeon General's report on mental health indicates a number of serious differences in the experiences of people from different ethnicities; in particular disparities in the quality and availability of access to mental health services (Dept. of Health and Human Services, 1999). The report tends to highlight disparities in service delivery, rather than fundamental differences in the severity or prevalence of mental illness among different ethnic groups. The report also indicates that although there are many effective treatments for mental illness, racial and ethnic minorities have less chance of experiencing quality care than the rest of the population. As a result, racial and ethnic minorities experience a much higher rate of disability from untreated or inadequately treated mental illness. Culture is another important factor in accessing mental health services, the report found. Culture influences the ways in which people communicate their symptoms to doctors and clinicians, how they cope, how they relate to their family and community, and also their preparedness to seek treatment. For some ethnic groups, their history of experiencing racism and discrimination (as well as poverty) means that they are less likely to trust health professionals. A lack of cultural sensitivity among health professionals may worsen such trust.

The social and economic position of African Americans is highlighted in the report as a risk factor for mental illness. For instance, African Americans are more likely to experience homelessness, incarceration, the child welfare system, and to be victims of trauma (all of which increase the risk of mental illness). Also, African Americans are more likely than Caucasians to experience mental disorders, with the data suggesting that socioeconomic position (rather than race, culture or ethnicity) being the cause of this disparity. Another important finding of the report was that African Americans are under-represented in terms of receiving outpatient services, but they are over-represented as inpatients in the public health system.

Many other ethnic groups also have significant unmet mental health needs. The report concluded that up to 40% of Hispanic Americans have limited English-language proficiency – and the inability of most mental health care providers to speak Spanish, and to understand Hispanic cultures, (as well as the low number of mental health providers who are themselves) means that Hispanic Americans may also find it hard to access quality mental health care. American Indians/Native Americans are another ethnic group who experience unique risks for certain types of mental illness. For instance, they have a suicide rate which is 50% higher than the national rate, and they also experience much higher rates of co-occurring mental illness and substance abuse (especially alcohol). Asian Americans and Pacific Islanders also have unique mental health risks. They seem to delay seeking mental health care (because of shame and stigma). So when they do finally seek help for mental illness, Asian Americans and Pacific Islanders tend to have far more severe mental health problems than other ethnic groups.

Another excellent source of information about health disparities is the book published by the National Academies Press called "Unequal Treatment: Confronting Racial and Ethnic Disparities in Health Care" (Smedley et al., 2003). The first paragraph of this book summarizes much of its evidence:

> Racial and ethnic minorities tend to receive a lower quality healthcare than non-minorities, even when access-related factors, such as patients' insurance and income, are controlled. The sources of these disparities are complex, are rooted in historic and contemporary inequities, and involve many participants at several levels, including health systems, their administrative and bureaucratic processes, utilization managers, healthcare professionals, and patients... Minorities may experience a range of other barriers to accessing care, even when insured at the same level as whites, including barriers of language, geography, and cultural familiarity. Further, financial and institutional arrangements of health systems, as well as the legal, regulatory, and policy environment in which they operate, may have disparate and negative effects on minorities' ability to attain quality care.

Some of the literature reviewed in this report is a scathing indictment on the healthcare system because it indicates:

- In psychiatric emergency services, African Americans are more likely to be given prescriptions for anti-psychotic medicines than other ethnic groups. 'Race' accounted for these differences, rather than the severity of their symptoms, their perceived dangerousness, their psychiatric history, etc;
- Caucasians were more likely to be given prescriptions for anti-depressants than African Americans;
- There are significant differences in coronary revascularization procedures which are often associated with higher mortality rates for African American people; and

- African Americans are far less likely than Caucasians to receive anti-retroviral therapies for the treatment of HIV.

Unfortunately, the report by the Institute of Medicine largely (though not exclusively) focused on the experiences of African American people, and under-reported the experiences of other ethnic groups. This point was highlighted in a fascinating article entitled "The Mental Health of Ethnic Minority Groups: Challenges posed by the Supplement to the Surgeon General's report on Mental Illness" (Sue & Chu, 2003). Sue and Chu argue that the prevalence of mental illness varies according to ethnicity – American Indians seem to have lower rates, Native Americans have higher rates, and Asian Americans and Pacific Islanders have the same (or a little lower) rates of mental illness than Caucasians. They suggest that what is needed is a focus on particular ethnic groups, and their specific experiences, rather than lumping all ethnic minorities together. Sue and Chu concur that differences in mental illness rates among different ethnic groups cannot be assumed to just reflect inequalities to access to services. They emphasize other complex mediating factors that can influence mental health, such as acculturation and adaptation strategies, racism, and cultural resources (support, networks, etc).

RESPONDING TO DISPARITIES

The Unequal Treatment report identified a number of strategies which could be implemented to address racial and ethnic disparities in healthcare, including an increase in the recruitment of ethnic minorities into the health professions, an emphasis on developing effective and culturally-competent health system via the use of interpreters and language-appropriate health educational materials, and an increase in education on cross-cultural issues for health care professionals (Smedley et al., 2003).

The *Unequal Treatment* report also recommends a number of strategies to reduce administrative and linguistic barriers to care including:

- Increasing awareness (both among the public and among healthcare providers) of the inequities which stem from healthcare disparities that result in negative outcomes for members of ethnic and linguistic minorities;

- Promoting changes in the behavior of minority patients who refuse treatment;
- Providing information in culturally appropriate ways so that it the responses to problems are effective, respectful and understandable;
- Increasing the employment rates of people from different linguistically and culturally diverse groups;
- Increasing awareness and expanded research into the importance of bias, stereotyping and clinical uncertainty in the patient-healthcare provider interaction;
- Ongoing cross-cultural training for all staff;
- The employment of bilingual staff and interpreters within healthcare organizations, at no cost to patients;
- Both verbal and written options being provided to patients in their preferred languages;
- Using competent, trained staff (rather than family or friends) as interpreters;
- Providing materials and signs in languages which reflect the ethnic composition of the local community;
- The incorporation of an awareness of cultural and linguistic diversity into strategic planning and organizational performance indicators;
- Using both formal and informal mechanisms for community consultation so that the diversity of the community is reflected in feedback mechanisms;
- Reducing the disparities which mean that people with different insurance levels receive different quality of healthcare;
- The development of stronger relationships between minority patients and doctors who understand the issues raised by cultural and linguistic diversity (because the doctors can, in some ways, become advocates for their patients);
- Applying the same sorts of protections for people covered by publicly-funded HMOs as people who are covered by privately-funded HMOs and also restructuring payment programs for healthcare providers to enhance service provision to minority patients;
- Utilizing community health workers (especially among medically underserved and ethnic minority populations) and as a liaison between healthcare providers and the communities they serve;

- Enforcing regulations about civil rights so that people have recourse when injustices occur; and
- Providing culturally appropriate patient education programs so that patients from linguistic and ethnic minorities can participate effectively in their treatment.

While these strategies to address racial and ethnic disparities in healthcare are no doubt thoughtful and will address some of the problems which members of ethnic minorities experience, they are nevertheless limited because they only address the healthcare context. Other issues outside the ambit of a healthcare context are perhaps equally important from a sociological perspective. Perhaps the most important omission from these recommendations is any type of strategy to address wider issues of racism in society, which affects income, wealth employment, housing, life expectancy, education, and various forms of social exclusion. The combined effect of all these forms of social exclusion and prejudice is that from the cradle to the grave, members of certain ethnic groups (for instance, African Americans) experience worse health and higher mortality rates than their Caucasian counterparts. African American people, for instance, have both higher infant mortality rates, and shorter life spans, than non-Hispanic Whites. To address the health disparities and higher mortality rates of African Americans, which have been highlighted in this chapter, some more profound social changes may need to occur.

Recognition of the impact of racism on health and illness is clearly important from a sociological perspective. And while the "Unequal Treatment" report does recognize the influence of bias, prejudice and stereotyping against minorities in clinical encounters, this is a very narrow approach towards racism. A more comprehensive sociological approach to racism would recognize all of its historical and contemporary implications – including its effects on housing, employment, poverty rates, insurance levels, and so on. Such a wholesale approach to redressing the effects of racism on the life chances of minority ethnic groups is conspicuously absent from the Unequal Treatment report.

Essentially, the Institute of Medicine has recommended strategies that aim to address disparities in health and illness only in the context of the medical system, and not in the wider community. Their strategies will undoubtedly result in greater awareness of disparities in the healthcare system and improved healthcare practices, but they do not suggest some of the wider social changes which may increase the social standing (and indirectly, the health and illness experiences) of ethnic minorities. For instance, higher employment rates may not only address those disabilities, diseases and illnesses which are more commonly associated with poverty, they could also be expected to improve the rates of insurance coverage for ethnic minorities.

"COLOR BLIND RACISM" AND "NEW RACISM"

While the above statistics can give some indication of the inequitable distribution of certain health conditions, and the unequal nature of barriers in the health care system, it is inadequate to simply acknowledge these disparities without placing them in a broader social context. This context, some sociologists believe, involves what is known as "color blind racism" (Bonilla-Silva, 2006). Another term for this form of racism is "new racism" (Hill Collins, 2006). "Color blind racism" is a term used to describe the structural and institutional inequalities experienced by minority ethnic groups – patterns of discrimination which mean that certain groups are consistently disadvantaged in a wide range of areas including employment, education, and health/illness. The term "color blind" is used to indicate that this persistent pattern may not be conscious at all – unlike the Civil Rights era, it typically involves more subtle forms of behavior, or policies and practices that seem non-discriminatory but actually deny equal opportunity to all members of all ethnic groups (Bonilla-Silva, 2006).

Unfortunately, many books in the field of disability studies regard 'race' or ethnicity as a non-issue (and ignore it altogether), or else they either relegate it to the status of a side-issue which only affects people from ethnic minorities (Barnes, Mercer, & Shakespeare, 2005; Longmore, 2003; Michalko, 2002). There are many problems with such an approach to the interconnections between disability and ethnicity, not the least of which is a failure to recognize that *everyone* who is disabled has a race or ethnicity. Likewise, as this chapter has indicated, every disability has a different demographic distribution. And the power dimensions which operate in society – forms of privilege as well as social marginalization – are not only implicated in the production of racism, sexism and other forms of social exclusion but are equally involved in the production, social distribution and response to illness, disease and disability. Hill Collins would suggeste that ignoringe the connections between race' and ethnicity and disease/illness/disability is a form of 'new racism'. Hill Collins comments that this new racism "claimed not to see race yet managed to replicate racial hierarchy as effectively as the racial segregation of the old" (Hill Collins, 2006).

Moreover, postcolonial literature has stressed the need to critically interrogate the taken-for-granted categories of ethnicity, through its emphasis on 'critical white studies'. This literature suggests a number of principles which should be applied to the connections between illness, disease, disability and ethnicity, including the realization that not only 'race', but ethnicity is also socially constructed. Identification with particular ethnic groups, for Caucasians, is heavily influenced by social class, age, parental ancestry and marital status (Waters, 1990). Critical white studies has also shown that the forms of privilege associated with being 'white' are not uniformly or evenly distributed (Lipsitz, 2006). This means that equal attention needs to be paid to different ethnic groups who are lumped together under the "White" umberella, as well as noting the importance of overlapping and intersecting identities such as class, age, gender, and other demographic characteristics. Hopefully, this book will contribute to such analysis.

Elsewhere I have written about the overlapping nature of discussions about disability and postcolonialism and their impact on discourses about the nation and citizenship rights (Sherry, 2007). What is particularly important to recognize is that discussions of disease, illness, disability and contamination are often underpinned by racist discourse (Farmer, 1993). However, they have also been highly gendered and have attempted to control reproduction and women's bodies in particular (Barlow, 2005) It is important to recognize the association of particular medical conditions with specific ethnic or racial groups, but it is equally important not to slip into discourses which are riddled with sexist or racist overtones in characterizing, or responding to disparities in the social distribution of health and illness.

Many discourses of 'contagion' and 'contamination' are underpinned by implicit (and occasionally explicit) racialized and ethnic prejudices. Indeed, the cultural construction of communicable diseases has a long history of fear, prejudice, chauvinism and xenophobia (Wald, 2008). This often amounts to apportioning a "geography of blame" – where a mixture of cultural misunderstanding, prejudice, fear, stereotype and accusation combine to blame certain cultures for particular diseases and epidemics (Farmer, 1993). Such themes have circulated in journalistic and scientific reports, novels and films, the mass media, and in many other arenas, constituting Wald calls the "outbreak narrative" (Wald, 2008). An integral part of this narrative is the stigmatization of particular locales, groups and behaviors, alongside the attribution of blame to these groups.

THE NEW GENOMICS AND "RACE"

One of the most important scientific developments of recent years has involved the draft mapping of the human genome – a potentially life-saving discovery which has the potential to provide new and exciting treatments for a range of human diseases and disabilities. However, the promise of this innovative approach to illness, disease and disability is often exaggerated, and the potential dangers are sometimes minimized among the hyperbole of marketing and promotion by drug research companies and others (Kerr & Shakespeare, 2002). Moreover, research into the human genome has been criticized for extending the medical gaze into particular ethnic populations – raising issues of governance, monitoring and surveillance of marginalized minorities. Indeed, the implications of human genetics for the concepts of 'race' and ethnicity are far from obvious because they may challenge long-standing ideas about shared biological inheritance (Pálsson, 2007).

The specter of eugenics haunts the new genetics in many ways – institutionally, discursively and politically. And yet the implications of human genetics for the concepts of 'race' and disability are far from obvious. Both the development of 'imagined communities' and assumptions about shared biological inheritance are in need of careful scrutiny, since they raise complex issues of identity, belonging, kinship, connection and citizenship. Such discussions cannot simply be reduced to "gene centrism" (Pálsson, 2007).

CONCLUSION

This chapter has highlighted a number of issues associated with racial and ethnic disparities in health, illness, disease and disability. It has demonstrated that disability and illness is unevenly distributed throughout the population and that ethnic minorities experience higher rates of some conditions, and much lower rates of others. It has also highlighted the fact that people from different ethnic groups who ostensibly have the same disability or illness may actually experience different disabling barriers. For instance, people with similar pain experiences can be given different medical treatments, because of their perceived 'race' or ethnicity. Moreover, the unequal social distribution of wealth and power, which itself is ethnicized, further contributes to the uneven quality of care that may influence the lives of people from different ethnic backgrounds. Finally, the chapter also identified various strategies to address some of these disparities.

Chapter 3

DISABILITY AND GENDER

This chapter explores some of the interconnections between gender and disability and provides some of the broad demographics of disability and gender in the USA. It begins with definitions of sex and gender and then discusses the way certain health conditions can complicate a person's sex/gender positioning. Again, differences in the incidence of particular disabilities among men and women are highlighted. The chapter identifies some of the gender-specific barriers which exist for disabled people in the healthcare system. Knowing about gender differences in various disorders, illnesses, and health conditions can help us to provide appropriate care and support, and also to develop appropriate prevention strategies. Additionally, the chapter highlights the ways gender intersects with many of the other identities that have been discussed in this book.

DEFINING SEX AND GENDER

For many years, the distinction has been made between 'sex' and 'gender'. These differences are well known, and are even incorporated into official policy documents. For instance, the World Health Organization has defined sex and gender in the following way (http://www.who.int/gender/whatisgender/en/index.html)

> *"Sex"* refers to the *biological and physiological* characteristics that *define* men and women. *"Gender"* refers to the *socially constructed* roles, behaviors, activities, and attributes that a given society *considers appropriate* for men and women. To put it another way: "male" and "female" are sex categories, while

"masculine" and "feminine" are gender categories. Aspects of sex will not vary substantially between different human societies, while aspects of gender may vary greatly.

Some examples of sex characteristics:

- Women can menstruate while men cannot.
- Men have testicles while women do not.
- Women have developed breasts that are usually capable of lactating, while men do not.
- Men generally have more massive bones than women.

Some examples of gender characteristics:

- In the United States (and most other countries), women earn significantly less money than men for similar work.
- In Viet Nam, many more men than women smoke, as female smoking has not traditionally been considered appropriate.
- In Saudi Arabia men are allowed to drive cars while women are not.
- In most of the world, women do more housework than men.

Perhaps you can see a problem with this quote, perhaps not. But there is a problem. It actually stems from the way people are lumped into two categories: EITHER men OR women. But… some people find themselves (because of the way they are born, or because of operations, or because of other factors) having real trouble with these categories. The case of people who are intersex – is a really good example of how health and illness experiences can complicate sex and gender!

INTERSEX

"Intersex" is a term used to describe someone who has an anatomy that is neither clearly male nor female. In the past, many intersexed people were labeled "hermaphrodites". However, the category of intersex includes many people who do not conform to the standard medical definitions of "hermaphroditism" - namely, having both ovarian and testicular tissue. It is actually more common among intersexed people for their genitals to be ambiguous, regardless of whether they have ovaries or testes. "Intersex" is actually a catch-all term which includes various conditions, such as Androgen Insensitivity Syndrome (which might result in a woman not having a uterus or ovaries), Klinefelter's Syndrome (which often means that a man has two X chromosomes and a Y chromosome, alongside smaller testicles and infertility), progestin induced virilization (which means that parental exposure to progestin can cause a female fetus to develop a phallus or to have a fused labia), mixed gonadal dysgenesis (where the development of gonads is abnormal and may only involve connective tissue), and true hermaphrodism (the presence of both male and female sex organs).

The intersex movement challenges dominant social interpretations of bodily differences, such as medical practices that define one penis as "too small", a clitoris as "too large", or the absence of a vagina as "not a real woman". The intersex movement generally objects to surgery unless it is absolutely medically necessary, such as a lifesaving operation in which a urethra is rerouted so that a child can urinate.

"Just How Sexually Dimorphic Are We?" is the name of a fascinating article which discusses the frequency of unusual sexual organs, as opposed to what it calls "the ideal male or female" (Blackless et al., 2000). This article reviews medical literature from 1955 to 2000 and estimated that 2% of live births do not fit the traditional binary of being "the ideal male or female". Of course, that does not mean that 2% of people have some sort of "sex correction" surgery – just that the percentages of people with unusual anatomies is far greater than is usually assumed. A note on the terminology is necessary, however. Even though these authors support increased awareness of the diversity of sexual anatomy, their reference to the categories "ideal male" and "ideal female" is itself problematic. Such terms notions have implicit normative standards based on gender, race, disability, age, and other factors.

So... it is important to preface any discussion of the issues of "men and women with particular health conditions" with a qualification – there are some health conditions that mean people don't neatly fit into this binary of 'men' or 'women'!

THE UNEVEN DISTRIBUTION OF DISABILITY AMONG MEN AND WOMEN

There are many surveys and reports on men and women with disabilities – each of which produce different estimates of the disability population (Altman, Barnartt, Hendershot, & Larson, 2003). Just for the purposes of beginning a discussion of the demographics of disability, this chapter will rely on the US Census to obtain some basic data about disability in the USA. Some of the basic statistics from this Census are summarized below. In 2000, over 49 million people in the US (19.3% of the population) were disabled. There were more disabled women than men (24,439,531 disabled men and 25,306,717 disabled women, according to these statistics). Also, the rate of disability increases with age: it is only 5.8% among people aged 5 to 15, but it climbs to 41.9% for people over 65 years of age. Interestingly, among younger people, there are MUCH higher rates of disability among boys age 5-15 years than among girls of the same age. The biggest difference in this age group can be found in the area of mental disabilities, where there are 1.3 million boys, and only 600,000 girls. As people get older, there are many more women with disabilities than men with disabilities. In every category of disability (sensory, physical, mental, self-care, and going outside the home) in the age group of people over 65, there are more women than men with disabilities. In the case of mental disabilities, the differences are profound: there are 2.2 million women over 65 who have a mental disability, compared to only 1.3 million. Likewise, when it comes to disabilities that affect self-care, there are 2.1 million women over the age of 65 with this disability, compared to only 1 million men.

Having discussed some of the broad statistics about the distribution of disability among men and women, it is now necessary to explore some particular diseases, illnesses and disabilities which are unevenly distributed among men and women. The first condition to be discussed is Post Traumatic Stress Disorder (PTSD). PTSD is a condition which develops in response to trauma, and often means that the person re-lives the event, and then persistently avoids reminders of the event. One simplistic way of reporting the data about PTSD would be to simply state that women report far higher rates of PTSD than men. A National Comorbidity Survey Report, which surveyed over 8,000 people, confirms this basic statistic (National Center for PTSD, 2005). The National Comorbidity Survey Report concluded "The estimated lifetime prevalence of PTSD among adult Americans is 7.8%, with women (10.4%) twice as likely as men (5%) to have PTSD at some point in their lives".

However, to simply report a higher incidence of PTSD among women may be true, but it really only paints half the picture. What is equally important to recognize is that the PTSD which men and women experience often stems from very different causes. To address the issues associated with women and PTSD, it is necessary to confront issues of domestic violence, rape, sexual molestation, physical attack, childhood physical abuse and being threatened with a weapon (PTSD). On the other hand, PTSD issues for men often involve combat exposure, childhood neglect, childhood physical abuse, and rape. So while both men and women reported PTSD from rape and childhood physical abuse, combat exposure was a far more common cause of PTSD for men than women, as was childhood neglect. And sexual molestation was a more common cause of PTSD in women, as was being threatened with a weapon. The different causes of PTSD among men and women are believed to result in more symptoms and longer, as well as more severe, effects for women (Seedat, Stein, & Carey, 2005). It is important to know about these differences, because to understand, prevent and respond appropriately it is important to be able to target resources in the most effective ways possible.

Another condition which is very unevenly distributed – according to both gender and ethnicity - is the experience of Migraine. One survey of over 12,000 people in Baltimore, Maryland, some research suggested that gender is an important factor in the prevalence of Migraine – women consistently report higher levels of Migraine than men (Stewart et al., 1996). Among Caucasian men, 8.7% reported Migraines, compared to 7.2% of African American men and 4.2% of Asian American men. These compared to 20.4% of Caucasian women who reported Migraines, 16.2% of African American women and 9.2% of Asian women who reported Migraines. As these statistics indicate, among African Americans and Asian Americans, there are much lower rates of Migraines compared to Migraines in Caucasians. This survey also suggested that we are not just talking about a difference in the actual rates of an illness or health condition among different ethnic groups, we are also talking about different degrees of severity. Although there were higher rates of headache pain reported by African Americans than among Caucasians and Asian Americans, but lower rates of nausea and vomiting. The authors concluded that the overall effects of Migraine reported by African Americans seemed to be less disabling than those reported by Asian Americans and Caucasians with Migraines.

Another disability which is marked by strong differences between men and women is Stroke. A Stroke involves a blood clot or a leakage of blood which interrupts the flow of blood to the brain. At each age, males are more at risk than females to *have* a Stroke, but women are more likely to *die* from a Stroke (T. Thom et al., 2006). The higher mortality rate of Stroke among women is caused by the fact that women live longer than men. Also, women who have a Stroke tend to be more disabled than men (Roquer, Campello, & Gomis, 2003). As well, women are more likely than men to have atypical Stroke symptoms (Labiche, Chan, Saldin, & Morgenstern, 2002). Furthermore, gender bias seems to affect cardiovascular testing – when they present with the same symptoms, men are more likely than women to receive cardiac catheterizations and stress tests (Chang et al., 2007). As well as gender, 'race' or ethnicity is a major risk factor for Stroke. African Americans are at higher risk of Stroke than other groups. Death rates from Strokes are approximately 3 or 4 times higher for African Americans than they are for Caucasians (Howard, Labarthe, Hu, Yoon, & Howard, 2007). African American men have a higher rate of Stroke than African American women, but they both have a higher rate than Caucasian men, who have a higher rate than Caucasian women. This increased risk is partly because of higher incidence of high blood pressure, diabetes and obesity (Ruland et al., 2003).

In general, there are major differences between men and women in terms of the onset, distribution and presentation of cardiovascular disease throughout the lifecourse (Ferrary & Jablonski, 2004). Premenopausal women only rarely experience Cardiovascular Diseases, whereas postmenopausal women experience these diseases far more often (Mendelsohn & Karas, 2005). Estrogen seems to have a protective role for heart disease among premenopausal women, but after menopause, the risk of heart attack increases significantly (especially if menopause is the result of surgery). Moreover, women tend to present with chest pain as their first system of cardiovascular disease, whereas men are more likely to present with a heart attack or sudden death. This difference is important because it means that coronary artery disease is more likely to be detected later in women than men (Ferrary & Jablonski, 2004).

Bipolar disorder also has marked gender differences. Bipolar disorder involves feelings of being excessively high (mania), and being very low (depression) and is best understood as a continuum, which could involve mild or severe effects. Women with bipolar disorder seem to have far more rapid cycling than men (Leibenluft, 1996). "Rapid cycling" means having quickly succeeding manic/depressive episodes, typically involving more than four manic/depressive episodes per year. Women who have Bipolar disorder also tend to have more depressive episodes (and fewer manic episodes) than men with bipolar disorder. Additionally, women are more likely to have a mixed form of mania, quite different from the mania experienced by men with Bipolar Disorder. In terms of the treatment of bipolar disorder among women, there are really interesting issues associated with pregnancy. For instance, it is well known that mood stabilizers are expressed through breast milk, and they may also affect the chances of having a child with "birth defects" (though many disability scholars think the language of "birth defects" is very problematic because it paints such a negative picture of the child). As a result, there needs to be a careful examination of both risks and benefits in making decisions about medication during pregnancy. This social element of decision making about medication – making a very personal decision about maternal and child health –underscores the importance of gender as a factor in the treatment of Bipolar disorder.

Chronic Obstructive Pulmonary Disease (COPD) is another disability with interesting gender dimensions. COPD refers to a group of respiratory tract diseases involving obstructed airflow, such as chronic bronchitis, emphysema, and bronchiectasis. Some of the causes of COPD include smoking and exposure to coal dust or solvents. COPD is usually permanent and progressive. Data from 2000 and earlier suggested that males had a higher incidence of COPD overall, though women had a higher rate among people who are over 70 years of age (Silverman et al., 2000). However, more recent data suggests that women now have a higher rate of COPD than men, perhaps because women are smoking far more now (Han et al., 2007). Additionally, recent studies suggest that women with COPD who are dependent on oxygen die at a faster rate than males (Machado et al., 2006). Furthermore, some studies suggest that women with COPD have higher rates of anxiety and depression than men with the same level of ventilatory impairment (Di Marcoa et al., 2006). Also (as with every chronic disease) the prevalence of COPD is strongly associated with age. Another interesting factor that increases the risk of developing COPD is lower socioeconomic status (Hegewald & Crapo, 2007). Once again, the evidence highlights the interaction of a diverse range of social factors with the incidence of disability. It also suggests that different policy and practice responses are required in targeting vulnerable groups – such as young women whose smoking rates seem to be moving in an opposite direction to young men.

A recent article also suggests that women and men also have different experiences of both sleep and sleep disorders. Although women report better sleep quality and longer sleep times than men, they also have more sleep-related complaints than men. Women experience higher rates of insomnia, and this difference between men and women increases with age. Also, women seem to have higher rates of restless leg syndrome whereas the rate of rapid eye movement sleep disorder is more common among men (Krishnan & Collop, 2006).

Osteoporosis is another disability which is far more common among women (particularly older women). This sex difference means that all postmenopausal women should be evaluated for signs of osteoporosis during routine physical examinations – and special attention should be given to those women who have known risk factors for osteoporosis, such as a personal or family history of hip fractures (Lane, 2006).

It is now time to turn to another disability – Alcoholism. Alcoholism is an experience that few people regard as a disability, but it actually is a psychiatric disability which has been recognized in the Diagnostic and Statistical Manual, the main diagnostic tool used by psychiatrists and psychologists, for many years. Like many other forms of mental illness, Alcoholism is a gendered disease – it occurs far more commonly among men than women. Also, it is widely believed that chemical differences exist in the ways men and women respond to effects of alcohol. However, scientific research on this topic has provided inconsistent results because of variations among each sex, which may be associated with the role of body composition, genetic factors, gastric and hepatic alcohol dehydrogenase, and gastric absorption (Thomasson, 1995). This scientific research is an important reminder of the need to be careful of making simplistic assumptions about sex and disability, given the diverse range of experiences within each sex.

The topic of Alcoholism also raises some interesting gender dynamics in terms of help-seeking behaviors. Some research published in the early 1990s found that men were more likely to seek treatment in alcohol-specific clinics whereas women were more likely to present at non-alcohol-specific clinics, such as mental health clinics or emergency health services (Weisner & Schmidt, 1992). This research also suggested that men have higher rates of Alcoholism than women, but women who presented for alcohol treatment had more severe symptoms than their male counterparts (Weisner & Schmidt, 1992). Some subsequent studies have confirmed that women are still more likely to visit mental health clinics only, rather than clinics which are specifically identified as alcohol-specific (Green-Hennessy, 2002). Differences in treatment preference may be connected to a perception that alcoholism, problem drinking and public intoxication by women is far more socially unacceptable than similar behavior by men (Gomberg, 1988). Similarly, there were significant gender differences – not only in terms of difficulty in seeking help, fear about being labeled an "alcoholic" or a "psychiatric patient", and the perceived social and family costs of seeking treatment – but also in terms of the influences of a spouse, and the ways in which people perceived the links between their alcohol problems and other aspects of their lives (B. Thom, 1986).

Parkinson's Disease is another disability with marked sex differences – more men develop it than women (though the difference reduces with age, presumably due to mortality), and yet women tend to report worse symptoms (Shulman, 2007). The progression of Parkinson's Disease in women is quite different than in men – and this is believed to be associated with sex differences in estrogen (Czlonkowska, Ciesielska, Gromadzka, & Kurkowska-Jastrzebska, 2005). However, the websites of Parkinson's disease organizations rarely mention such issues – instead they tend to simply list symptoms such as tremors, slowness of motion, or balance problems.

The case of Multiple Sclerosis (MS), which was briefly discussed in Chapter One, is another neurological disability which has well-known sex differences. But what is less commonly known is that gender is a risk factor for all autoimmune disorders – with women experiencing almost 80% of such diseases (Gleicher & Barad, 2007). Some other examples of autoimmune disorders that women experience more than men include Lupus (a multi-organ disorder that can affect musculoskeletal, neuropsychiatric, ocular, and renal systems), Hypothyroidism (which often involves hair loss, weight gain, temperature intolerance, and lethargy), Rheumatoid arthritis (a chronic inflammation of the joints) and SjöGren's Syndrome (where the mouth and eyes become extremely dry). The cause of this sex discrepancy is not entirely clear, although sex hormones and genetics are thought to play a role in the process of developing autoimmune diseases (Gleicher & Barad, 2007). Such data on sex differences in autoimmune diseases is not simply interesting anecdotally – it means that women MUST be significantly represented in any community consultations and policy development concerning such diseases.

This brief review of some of the important biological differences between men and women which lead to differences in the incidence of particular disabilities is important because it suggests that such biological differences need to be thoroughly investigated in order to develop appropriate responses. A 2001 report by The Institute of Medicine entitled "Exploring the biological contributions to human health: does sex matter?" (Wizemann & Pardue, 2001), it was suggested that there is not nearly enough research done on the ways in which sex-specific and biological differences influence overall health. This is important, because any perspective which ignores the issue of sex and biological difference provides only a partial picture of a complex problem.

Of course it would be faulty to assume that biological reasons alone explain the differences between the incidence of particular diseases, disorders, disabilities and health conditions between men and women. To fully explore the interaction of gender and disability, or the ways in which certain barriers in the healthcare system might address the needs of one sex ahead of another, it is necessary to examine how some social institutions are more or less receptive to the needs of men, or women. In doing so, it is important to examine many factors, including the importance of gender as a risk factor for the development of a certain disabilities or health conditions and strategies reduce the incidence of gender-specific barriers or gender disparities in health and disability.

GENDER AS A RISK FACTOR

Many social structures are consciously gendered in very specific ways (such as restaurants that only hire female waitresses or security firms that only hire male security guards). Sometimes, the connections are implicit rather than explicit – they rely more on unspoken assumptions about gender roles to act as an informal regulation mechanism. But to explain the connections between disability and gender, it is necessary to recognize that gender roles influence patterns of behavior which may create certain disabilities more commonly in one sex as opposed to another.

Gender is deeply connected with the incidence of disability. For instance, the world of work is highly gendered - and the process of men (or women) dominating the workforce in particular industries contributes significantly to the differences in disability rates. Classic examples include the connection between arthritis or repetitive strain injury in the hand and secretarial work (a field dominated by women). But the risks of injury or disability for female workers are not confined to office workers. Indeed, a recent study suggests that women who work in the following industries all experience a high risk of an injury which requires hospitalization:

- Cleaning, laundries and dry cleaners,
- Transport of passengers,
- Hotels and restaurants,
- Hospitals, and
- Transport of goods (Kines, Hannerz, Mikkelsen, & Tüchsen, 2006).

Additionally, nursing (another female-dominated profession) has the highest work-related incidence of any profession (Nelson, Fragala, & Menzel, 2006).

Carpel Tunnel Syndrome is another case where women have much higher rates of injury than men – women experience this problem three times as often as men. It has been suggested that the cause of this discrepancy is the way women are often allocated high-risk tasks within high-risk industries (McDiarmida, Olivera, Ruserb, & Gucera, 2000). Unfortunately, the relationship between such industrial injuries, disability and gender has been historically neglected. Some of the effects of this neglect include lack of attention to the specific occupational hazards and health problems, failure to analyze the relationship between gender segregation and injuries/hazards in the labor market, and lack of analysis of domestic work hazards on injury, disease and disability (Artazcoz, Borrell, Cortàs, Escribà-Agüir, & Cascant, 2007).

Particular conceptions of gender may also contribute to the creation of disability. As an example, it is important to recognize the ways in which ideas about masculinity, toughness and men's bodies can contribute to risk-taking in certain areas which lead to higher rates of certain disabilities among men, such as Traumatic Brain Injury and Spinal Cord Injury (Connell, 2005).

A sociological examination of gender and disability also requires an examination of the issue of the medicalization of both masculinity (Rosenfeld & Faircloth, 2006) and femininity (Zimmermann, 1998). For instance, the medicalization of sexual intercourse – and the creation of diagnoses such as 'erectile disorder' and 'sexual dysfunction' – is an important reminder of the ways in which medical discourses interact with gender.

There is a potential trap in discussions of gender, disability, and medicine involving an unconscious move away from discussing gender – as a form of power relations between men and women – to instead focus on the specific ways in which the system of power associated with gender disadvantages women. In terms of a sociological perspective, such a narrow approach is very problematic for a number of reasons. First, we all have multiple identities – and some of the other identities which we have (for instance, ethnicity) may play a major role in the likelihood of acquiring a disability, and may also significantly influence how we are treated as a result. Gender relations are not all about sexism directed towards women – sophisticated analyses of gender relations to recognize overall inequities in power relationships between men and women, but they do far more than that as well. Gender is a multi-layered system of power, intersecting with many other layers of power (such as racism, ageism, and so on).

It is therefore important to specifically include men's health/illness/disease/disability experiences, and the ways they intersect with multiple identities, to balance out any discussion of gender. The theme of how men's attitudes about masculinity affect their relationship to health conditions is the theme of a fascinating article entitled "Constructions of masculinity and their influence on men's well-being: a theory of gender and health" (Courtenay, 2000). Importantly, the article also stresses that other identities such as ethnicity, economic status, education level, sexual orientation and other factors also influence the ways in which men perform their masculinity, and that all these factors have an effect on their overall health and wellbeing.

Men's health/illness/disease/disability must be understood from the perspective of gender relations, so that appropriate interventions can be designed. A gendered relations approach does not study men (or women) in isolation – the power relations between men and women, as well as the differences between men (and between women) also must be examined carefully. Not all men, or all women, share the same resources, cultural capital, or power – and this must be recognized in order to develop a sophisticated sociological understanding of the relationship between gender and other forms of power. For instance, indigenous men, men from non-English speaking backgrounds, African American men, men with disabilities, men or low socioeconomic status, and rural men can all be positioned as men with "special needs" – which means that their concerns are not included in the mainstream understanding of "men's health" (Schofield, Connell, Walker, Wood, & Butland, 2000).

An excellent book by Sarah Payne called "The Health of Men and Women" emphasizes that there are particular sub-groups of men and women who are especially vulnerable to certain diseases/illnesses/conditions and that by lumping all men together, or all women together, we may miss some important dynamics and patterns of inequality (Payne, 2006). For instance, she says that the overall picture of men dying earlier, but women getting sicker, is too broad. It is necessary to acknowledge that particular groups of men can experience much higher rates of illness/disease than women. Payne also stresses that there is a need to identify the specific conditions where men and women experience very different health outcomes. This was part of the reason I began this chapter with a long discussion of differences in conditions such as multiple sclerosis, Parkinson's disease, and so on – sophisticated analyses, such as those offered by Payne, are increasingly emphasizing the need to design strategies to reduce discrepancies in specific conditions.

Nevertheless, Payne provides a model of the relationship between sex, gender and health which is incredibly useful. It has four elements:

1. Identifying sex differences in particular conditions;
2. Identifying "structural/material factors" (in power, money, access to resources, work, and so on) which make men or women particularly vulnerable.
3. Examining the "gender discourses" (such as ideas about appropriate behaviors for men and women) which influence particular behaviors that might put someone at risk for developing a health condition; and
4. Developing more appropriate strategies for treatment and research.

Another important aspect of Payne's approach to health/illness is that she believes that we shouldn't emphasize men's health, or women's health, at the expense of the other. Payne recognizes that there are differences between men's and women's experiences at all levels of the healthcare system – from disease patterns to risk factors, medical knowledge, help-seeking behaviors and healthcare delivery. But she stresses that both require understanding of sex-specific differences, gender-sensitive policies, and an understanding of the gendered nature of health and healthcare.

I would now like to move on from Payne's book to another important issue – the ways in which other forms of social inequality can contribute to sex/gender differences in health and health care. I am concerned that we should not treat sex or gender as if they are the only identities people have – we all have an age, socioeconomic position, ethnicity, and so on... and each of these demographic factors can also contribute to whether we experience particular illnesses and conditions, and can also be a factor in determining whether we experience barriers in the healthcare system.

An example of the value of such an approach can be found in the experiences of men and women who have a heart attack, coronary heart disease or congestive heart failure in association with other illnesses such diabetes, hypertension and end-stage renal disease. Men and women have markedly different mortality rates from coronary heart disease – the reported mortality rate for African American men is 250.6 per 100,000, compared to 220.5 for White men, 169.7 for African American women, and 131.2 for Caucasian women (Correa-de-Araujo et al., 2006). It is obviously important to recognize these differences between different groups of men and women in order to develop appropriate responses and prevention strategies.

I will now use the example of the barriers in the healthcare system experienced by members of ethnic minorities as a supplement to the picture of sex/gender and health we have already developed. This is an area where Payne's model seems rather weak – but it is possible to supplement it and strengthen the model by recognizing multiple identities, as well as gender. As a part of addressing gender inequalities in healthcare, it is often necessary to challenge other inequalities also, such as barriers experienced by racial or ethnic minorities. Because everyone has multiple identities, they are not an 'add-on' which we should only consider when we think of minorities or special interest groups. Since everyone has many identities, thinking about multiple identities should be considered an 'ordinary' part of good professional practice.

GENDER-SPECIFIC BARRIERS IN THE HEALTHCARE SYSTEM

In order to identify what gender-specific barriers exist in the healthcare system, it is important to examine many issues, such as:

- Barriers at the system-level, such as differences between men and women in terms of having a usual source of care, health insurance, and problems with Medicaid/Medicare;
- The ways in which gender biases, stereotypes or prejudices might influence the subjective interpretation of symptoms in clinical settings;
- Investigating whether the under-employment of women (or men) in particular health and allied health professions might reduce awareness of the diversity of possible conditions, treatment options;
- Gaps in the training and education of health professions in terms of sex and gender; and
- Differences in help-seeking behaviors between men and women.

To identify some of the system-level barriers in healthcare system, I will begin by discussing some of the findings of *Health USA 2007,* the data book which is published by U.S. Department of Health and Human Services, Health Resources and Services Administration (HRSA).   It is interesting that this Government organization publishes data about "women's health", but does not publish similar information on "men's health". From a gender perspective, this omission is deeply problematic. Men, as well as women, have vulnerabilities associated with both sex and gender – and yet their specific needs are often ignored in health policies. Regardless, the Health USA 2007 data is important, and I will use it as a springboard for this discussion. As of Monday, July 28, 2008, *Health USA 2007* can be found at http://mchb.hrsa.gov/whusa_07/index.htm. Some of the barriers in the healthcare system which the data book identifies include differences between men and women in terms of having a usual source of care,   having   health   insurance,   and   experiencing   problems   with Medicaid/Medicare. I will expand on some of these issues shortly. But I want to recognize, at the outset, that this website focuses on women and there is a need to address men's health issues also.

Having a usual source of care and an established relationship with a physician has a number of health benefits, ranging from prevention of diseases to lower rates of subsequent hospitalization. According to the *Health USA 2007 data,* approximately 90% of women in the US have a regular healthcare provider, but poorer women are more likely to consider the Emergency Room their usual source of care. Obviously, this greatly increases costs and reduces the changes of them receiving preventative care. Lack of insurance is also associated with worse overall health. There were over 44 million uninsured people in the US in 2005. More men than women were uninsured – with the biggest discrepancy in the 18-24 year age group, where 32% of men, compared with 26% of women, were uninsured. In terms of our focus on gendered barriers – it seems that lack of health insurance is a major healthcare barrier for men. Interestingly, however, it is rarely framed in terms of "men's health"! Importantly, however, the majority of people on both Medicaid and Medicare are women. And the problems that people experience with these systems are well known. Despite the increasing costs of these programs, they seem to be characterized by a lack of effectiveness in providing quality care because of low reimbursement rates and excessive bureaucracy (Nenner, 1994). Additionally, people on these programs often report that they are unable to access a full range of treatments, services or medications and also that they experience long delays in obtaining treatment (Nenner, 1994).

There are also gendered barriers in insurance. Of course, both women and men have a range of problematic experiences with managed care - but that these are different problems. Often they are gendered problems. One study reported that women had more problems overall than men with the managed care system, in particular problems with closed networks of providers and gatekeepers to specialty care, but men had more problems with other practices, such as the requirement to be seeing a primary care provider (Mitchell & Schlesinger, 2005).

There are many more barriers in the healthcare system which *Health USA 2007* does not explore. One of the important areas which it ignored was the issue of sexism in medicine. To examine sexism in medical practice, a much better resource is Carole Thomas' article entitled "Medicine, Gender and Disability: Disabled Women's Health Care Experiences (Thomas, 2001). This article is interesting because of the ways it highlights both disablism (prejudice against people with disabilities) and sexism at the same time. Thomas summarizes existing literature which suggests that women experience sexism in medicine in various forms, including: the priorities set for medical research, the types of healthcare available, and in interpersonal interactions with health professionals. Another interesting element of Thomas' research is the way that disabled women are positioned as "trouble" or "unusual" patients because of their position as both women and disabled.

The extent to which women in medical schools also experience forms of sexism and sexual harassment is also the focus of a report entitled "Enhancing the Environment for Women in Academic Medicine" published by the Association of American Medical Colleges (Bickel, 1996). The study reports that over half of graduating seniors in medicine felt that the interaction of pharmokenetics (prescription drugs) and their different impact on men and women had been inadequately covered in their education. It seems that men are often used as the prototype for medical teaching. Furthermore, in terms of prejudice within medical schools, the Association of American Medical Colleges reported that many women in medicine have experienced sexism, and even come to adopt sexist prejudices or ways of behaving themselves.

Clinical trials have often been undertaken without sufficient regard to the different impacts which a drug might have on men and women. For instance, until recently there was no mandate requiring cardiovascular drugs to be tested on women as well as men – even thought cardiovascular disease is a major killer of women in the US (Spencer & Wingate, 2005). This failure to examine sex differences in pharmaceuticals is particularly dangerous given that a number of studies report it that adverse drug reactions are more common among women than men. One author suggests that women are between 1.5 and 1.7 times more likely than men to have an adverse drug reaction (Rademaker, 2001).

Another important gendered difference in healthcare involves help-seeking behaviors for medical concerns. There is a popular conception that women are more likely to seek help for health-related problems, which is reiterated in some medical sociology literature. For instance, according to Weiss and Lonnquist (2006: 45):

> Women perceive more symptoms, take them more seriously, and are more willing to see a physician about them. They are more likely to have a regular source of medical care, to use preventative care, to see physicians more often, to be prescribed medications, and to be hospitalized... Often, men would benefit from earlier and increased medical attention as a means of earlier diagnosis and intervention into diseases that become life threatening.

This quote helps to identify one key gendered area – help seeking behavior – which may influence the health and illness experiences of men and women. If we could change these gendered behaviors, then the chances of people developing certain illnesses, diseases, or disorders would be reduced; or their severity would be reduced. However, there is an important qualification which needs to be made to such arguments. A recent meta-review of literature on help-seeking behavior suggest that a more complex pattern of behavior actually exists: in some circumstances, women are more likely to seek help, in some cases men are, and in some cases, help-seeking behaviors were similar among men and women (Galdas, Cheater, & Marshall, 2005). Therefore it is necessary to investigate in far more detail which specific symptoms, illnesses and disabilities are most likely to involve resistance from men and women to seek medical assistance.

THE INTERSECTION OF MULTIPLE IDENTITIES – AND MULTIPLE BARRIERS

It is tempting to look at the issue of "gender" separately from every other identity. But of course, every identity we have – whether it is gender, age, ethnicity, sexuality, or anything else – occurs alongside other identities. That is how diversity operates in people's lives. And that means when we identify gendered healthcare barriers, we need to be mindful of how gender is related to other identities as well.

The following discussion will rely heavily on two articles by Bridget Read and Jen'nan Ghazal Gorman which analyze the health status of men and women in the United States according to 'race'/ethnicity and socioeconomic status (Read and Gorman 2006; Gorman and Read 2006). These articles are noteworthy in many respects, and deserve detailed examination. Interestingly, while the authors use the problematic racial terms 'black' and 'white', they have a far more nuanced and sophisticated approach to the 'Hispanic' category. Instead of using the racial term 'Hispanic', they use the language of ethnicity, such as 'Mexicans', 'Puerto Ricans', and 'Cubans'. (One can only regret that this level of sophistication was not applied to other categories that rely on the language of 'race' – such as 'black' and 'white'). The idea of disaggregating the category of "Hispanics" into three different groups is a good one because it avoids the problems associated with masking health disparities among different groups within this broad umbrella term.

For many years, medical sociologists have studied the reasons why women live longer, but have worse health than men. Gorman and Read suggest that the unequal distribution of economic and social resources plays an important role in creating such health disparities. For instance, lack of socioeconomic resources tends to be associated with higher forms of stress, and higher forms of both physical and mental disability. The fact that more men occupy higher socioeconomic status, and women experience worse socioeconomic outcomes, means that women may be exposed to a higher risk of disability. This article complicates the picture of gender and disability by emphasizing the differences that develop across the lifespan: males have a significant advantage early in the lifespan, but tend to develop higher rates of fatal diseases later in life, whereas women tend to develop higher rates of nonfatal diseases later in life.

Read and Gorman's article is particularly interesting because it has a combined focus on gender, ethnicity, and socioeconomic status (as well as many other factors) (Read & Gorman, 2006). They utilize data from the 1997-2001 National Health Interview Survey (NHIS), and examine topics such as men and women's self-rated health, functional limitations, and life-threatening medical conditions. While differences in socioeconomic status might explain variations between different ethnic groups, it does not explain why women would report worse health than men in the same ethnic group. And yet Read and Gorman note that *in all racial/ethnic groups, women have higher rates of functional limitations than men*. They also demonstrate that *there are huge differences between women, according to ethnicity, and also socioeconomic status*. The patterns of health inequalities, however, are not as simple as might first be assumed: for instance, while Mexican Americans experience lower socioeconomic outcomes, they report better health outcomes (in terms of morbidity and mortality rates).

Read and Gorman indicate that overall, both male and female members of all ethnic minorities are more likely than Caucasian men to report fair to poor health. (They use the problematic racial language 'white' for Caucasian, and 'black' for African American, but the following discussion will substitute these terms instead). In terms of this particular measure – self reported fair to poor health – the results are that Puerto Rican women have the worst outcomes, followed by Puerto Rican men, then African American men and women. On the other hand, Read and Gorman state that Caucasian men and women do not report significant differences in their self-reported health. (When these figures are actually adjusted for socioeconomic differences, however, Puerto Rican women are less likely to report problems with self-reported health, long term medical conditions, and functional limitations as compared with whites at the same level of income).

The data reviewed by Read and Gorman is quite remarkable in terms of demonstrating that overall, women have poorer health than men. They have:

- Higher rates of "functional limitations" than men (37% for women compared to 27% for men);
- Worse rates of self-reported poor/fair health (women with 12%, men with 10.5%); and

- Higher rates of long term medical conditions (34% female compared to 31% male).

There are bigger (and smaller) gender disparities within some ethnic groups compared to others. For instance, 26% of Cuban men, compared with 36% of Cuban women, have experienced a life threatening medical condition – whereas the rates of life threatening medical conditions are 30.6 % for Puerto Rican women and 30.1% for Puerto Rican men.

Women live longer than men – Read and Gorman state that in the United States in 2003, overall life expectancy for women was 80 years, compared to 74 years for men. Such data reflects the paradox that men die earlier, but women get sicker. Furthermore, Read and Gorman indicate that across the board, women have higher levels of functional limitation (one measure of disability) than men in the same ethnic groups. They also make an interesting observation in passing – men's health tends to increase much more than women's when the person is married, and it suggests that the reason for these differences is because men reduce their risky behavior and have more social support, whereas the benefits to women tend to be associated with higher income. Furthermore, levels of family support and social networks (both of which affect health) are different for men and women from different ethnic groups.

In another article, Gorman and Read note that work, and socioeconomic status, have a huge impact on the health and illness of men and women (Gorman & Read, 2006). The complex relationship between work and gender therefore also impacts health – women have more part-time work, tend to work in lower paid jobs, often get paid lower wages for the same work, and also perform a lot of unpaid work. And poorer socioeconomic status tends to be correlated with worse health, and less emotional resources (higher rates of depression, etc) with which a person can deal with these problems. These socioeconomic issues, which impact on men and women differently, impact significantly on overall health, illness and disability. Additionally, when reviewing the impact of racial/ethnic identities on health, illness and disability, Read and Gorman make another important comment – residential racial segregation impacts significantly on health because it effects health care access, opportunities for health improvement (e.g. exercise), increased exposure to unhealthy behaviors (e.g. smoking) and also increased stress.

Gorman and Read emphasize that women's health is a "kaleidoscope" which is influenced by factors such as ethnic background, socioeconomic status, and age, and that different measures of health problems produce different results. When it comes to functional limitations, there is a consistent picture of women's disadvantage – and this highlights the need for health policy initiatives which focus on reducing these particular disparities. Their work reminds us that it is sometimes misleading to generalize about the connections between health/illness/disability and gender without considering other factors such as ethnicity. For instance, different ethnic groups of women (and men) can have greatly different health status than others. Hence, addressing ethnic disparities in health is absolutely related to addressing gender disparities. Likewise, different measures of health/illness/disability status need to be examined, in determining priorities for health reform. Different measures of health/illness/disability can provide quite different results and point to different directions for policy reform and health improvement initiatives.

This discussion has therefore identified a number of recommendations for addressing gender disparities in health:

- Ensure that gender data is analyzed in terms of many demographic variables, including socioeconomic status, ethnicity, age, health behaviors and other factors;
- Use a number of different measures of health/illness/disability;
- Examine gender differences both among different ethnic groups, and within a particular ethnic group;
- Recognize the ways in which the gendered world of work and relationships impact on people's health, and therefore to explore the ways that changes could be promoted in these fields which would result in improved health outcomes;
- Explore ways of improving poorer people's socioeconomic status as a way of improving their health;
- Address the pattern of residential racial segregation as a way of improving health;
- Examine options for increasing health care access as a way of addressing the interaction of gender, race, poverty and ill health;
- Consider changes in the world of work (such as addressing the over-representation of women in unpaid work, and in poorer paying jobs) as one way of improving overall health rates;
- Examine the ways in which marriage promotes better health, and to examine what sorts of public health policies could support such initiatives;
- Ensure consultation processes are inclusive of (and attentive to the needs of) people from all ethnic groups, genders, socioeconomic backgrounds, and ages; and

- Identify the need for tailored health care responses to particularly underserved/needy groups in the community.

TARGETED INTERVENTIONS

The article which I will use as the basis for this discussion is entitled "Financing Health Care for Women with Disabilities" (Blanchard & Hosek, 2003). The report suggests that women with disabilities often have unique experiences in dealing with the healthcare system:

- Healthcare interventions often focus on their disabilities, but ignore their needs as women (such as the need to address reproductive health issues);
- There may be unique costs associated with disability-related issues (such as the need for non-standardized equipment) that are not covered under existing healthcare financing arrangements; and
- Certain operational practices within Medicare (such as its risk assessing procedures and its policies on coordinated care) may disadvantage women with disabilities.

The report also makes a number of important recommendations, such as training for primary care providers in the unique needs of disabled women (including providing information about their equipment).

In terms of other policy recommendations, the report suggests a need to incorporate a focus on prevention, as well as treatment; research both cost issues and the effectiveness of coordinated care programs integrated programs and specialized programs; and examine how health care financing and policy impact on this group. These issues – identifying the specific disadvantages experienced by particular groups of people, examining the policy, procedural and social barriers which affect their health, and then devising effective responses – underpin the rationale for tailored health interventions. The broad framework used in this report – consulting with key stakeholders, examining policy options, identifying areas for further research, and developing a multi-dimensional response to the health disparities which a particular group experiences – is the process that is undertaken whenever policies are developed in response to the needs of a disadvantaged population with specific or unique health, illness or disability needs. Of course, the barriers which people with specific illnesses, diseases, disorders and disabilities should be acknowledged and addressed. But the discussion in this chapter has also shown the dangers of misrepresenting problems experienced by people with a narrow range of conditions, disorders or disabilities as if they were experienced by all "people with disabilities".

The report by Blanchard and Hosek is a good example of this problem. Their report is entitled "Financing Health Care for Women with Disabilities", but their focus is far narrower than might at first be assumed. They admit in the Executive Summary of their report that they focus "primarily on women with physical/sensory disabilities under the age of 65". And yet, the demographic material they cite, which indicates that roughly one in five people is disabled – is inflated by the inclusion of many other disabilities/illnesses/disorders (such as learning disabilities, psychiatric disabilities, autoimmune diseases, heart diseases, etc), as well as older people (who have the highest rates of disability). This example, alone, demonstrates the need for critical examination of the exclusions which often take place in disability advocacy. This reductionist approach, which narrows the broad category of "disability" down to a much smaller number of physical or sensory conditions, is not restricted to the work of Blanchard and Hosek. It is, unfortunately, very common in disability studies (Sherry, 2006).

It is important to acknowledge that there is often a tension in health policy between focusing on the experiences of a particular group and developing interventions specifically aimed at them – for instance, disabled women – and developing a more general or universal policy on an issue such as insurance coverage, or universal coverage for everyone with a particular disease, disability or illness. Tailored interventions are often justified by saying that particular groups are not having their needs met, or are under-served in the current climate. Another rationale for tailored interventions is that it is necessary to identify the specific disadvantages experienced by particular groups of people, examining the policy, procedural and social barriers which affect their health, and then devise specific responses to the problem.

CONCLUSION

This chapter has continued the theme of the book that disability/disease/illness is an incredibly diverse experience, which is unevenly distributed among the population. It has shown that disability/disease/illness is unevenly distributed among men and women, and has also highlighted the way gender is a risk factor for certain disabilities. Some of the gender-specific barriers in the healthcare system have also been identified. And the chapter has highlighted the ways that people's multiple identities place them at different risk for developing certain diseases/disorders/illnesses. Another of these multiple identities – socioeconomic status – is the focus of the next chapter.

Chapter 4

DISABILITY AND SOCIOCONOMIC STATUS

This chapter will discuss the relationship between socioeconomic status and disability. It will begin by defining socioeconomic status and will then examine some disabilities which demonstrate remarkable disparities according to socioeconomic status. Then the chapter will examine the barriers which people experience because of socioeconomic status, and examine some options for barrier removal.

DEFINING SOCIOECONOMIC STATUS

Sociologists have spent a great deal of energy examining the patterns of inequality which exist in the US in terms of income, wealth and opportunity. They have shown that while there have been consistent patterns of inequality, changes certainly have occurred over time. These changes include the growing inequality between the rich and poor, as well as the increased concentration of wealth by the 'super-rich' relative to other high-income earners (Neckerman & Torche, 2007).

The relationship between the unequal distribution of wealth, income and opportunity and experiences of illness or disability has also been a central component of sociological research. Most research in the field has measure these inequalities through an implicit Weberian approach to social inequality, preferring the term "socioeconomic status" to the more Marxian discourse of "class". Nevertheless, whether the term "socioeconomic status" or "class" is used, it is abundantly clear that there is a strong connection between social position, health and illness - this is one of the most consistent findings of medical sociology. Studies have confirmed this relationship regardless of whether they have used income, education, or occupation as the indicator of social standing (Minkler, Fuller-Thomson, & Guralnik, 2006).

The term "socioeconomic status" is a broad term which seeks to combine both social and economic indicators of a person's standing in society. Because it is a broad term, there are many different measures of socioeconomic status, including household or family income, poverty status, social status, type of occupation, personal wealth, level of education, and so on. Occasionally, area-based measures of local social, economic and environmental resources have been used to provide a population-level analysis of health and socioeconomic position.

As indicated above, sociological research on class and socioeconomic status tends to be divided between Weberian approaches (which regard social position as an amalgam of class, status and power) and Marxist approaches (which tend to emphasize the primacy of class location and focus on antagonistic class relations). Eric Olin Wright has been a leading sociological theorist with regard to class and socioeconomic status, and has developed an innovative sociological approach to understanding class which attempts to combine some of the best features of Marxist and Weberian theories (Wright, 2000). Wright identified a number of difficulties in comparing and quantifying the experience of class on a cross-national basis. Wright indicates that his challenge was to use class analysis to explain why various capitalist countries displayed significant class differences:

- Differences in how rigid or permeable the class boundaries are;
- The different ways class location and class biography effect class consciousness in various countries; and
- The differences in ideologies of class across various countries.

Wright suggests that instead of viewing class as a simple, binary experience, it is important to recognize the complexity of contradictory and mediated class locations; privileges associated with skill, expertise and authority; the interaction of class with other social structures such as race and gender, including their influence on micro-level social interactions such as friendship and marriage; disjunctures that result from privileged and contradictory experiences such as capitalist assets owned by employees; and the temporal dimensions of class.

Unfortunately, such a sophisticated approach to class and socioeconomic status has rarely been applied in the literature on disability/disease/illness experiences. Instead, there are often very simplistic proxies used for class or socioeconomic status. Choosing a particular proxy as a marker of 'class' can result in markedly different results in terms of the relationship between socioeconomic position and health/illness/disability (Turrell, Hewitt, Patterson, &

Oldenburg, 2003). Even those studies which use a combination of factors such as education, occupation and household income are usually a long way from the theoretical sophistication offered by Wright.

In research on health and illness, some definitions of "socioeconomic status" place different emphasis on a person's income and assets whereas other definitions put more emphasis on social status or "prestige" (Bradley & Corwyn, 2002). Those that emphasize social status sometimes rely on a (modified) version of the work of Pierre Bourdieu and his notion of social, cultural, and economic capital to measure socioeconomic status. "Capital", in this sense, refers to those resources and assets available to a person. For Bradley and Corwyn, capital has many forms, including:

- "Financial capital" (things like income or access to financial resources);
- "Human capital" (someone's personal resources and qualifications such as education);
- "Social capital" (such as social connections, networks, "old boys clubs", etc).

There are, of course, immense problems operationalizing a variable such as "human capital" or "social capital" for research in the field of health and illness. So the approach by Bradley and Corwyn may not be as useful as it first appears. Nevertheless, their work is another reminder that socioeconomic status (or 'class' in the language of Marx and Wright) must be understood as a multi-faceted dynamic. Even those studies which rely on a combination of income, education and occupation as markers of socioeconomic status are still merely approximating this complex phenomenon.

Having said that, it is nevertheless evident that lack of material resources, and lack of community resources, greatly impacts on the experience of health/illness/disease/disability. The next section of this chapter will outline some of this evidence.

DISABILITY AND SOCIOECONOMIC STATUS

From the uterus to the cradle to the grave, being poor increases the risk of disease, disability and illness, and also increases mortality rates. Of course, not all illnesses are caused by socioeconomic status, and low socioeconomic status does not increase the risk of *all* illnesses, injuries and disabilities. Furthermore, socioeconomic status has behavioral, biological, psychological and social effects, all of which influence health and illness, and contribute to death rates. Nevertheless, as a general rule, poorer socioeconomic status increases the chances of becoming ill, experiencing disability, and dying at an earlier age. One recent article claimed that the gap between the mortality rates of the most affluent and the poorest sectors of US society is actually increasing, and the mortality rate for children from low-income families is 2 to 3 times higher than for children in high-income families (Singh & Kogan, 2007). Simply because of socioeconomic status, poorer people are estimated to have between 20 and 25% lower life expectancies than their wealthier counterparts (Wilkinson, 2005).

There are many illnesses and disabilities which are much more prevalent among lower socioeconomic groups. One obvious example is Cerebral Palsy, which is more common in poorer socioeconomic areas and which is often associated with a lower birth weight, itself influenced by social class (Odding, Roebroeck, & Stam, 2006), (Yeargin-Allsopp et al., 2008). This connection between lower birth weight and gestational age does not, however, entirely explain the strong association between socioeconomic status and the risk of Cerebral Palsy (Sundrum, Logan, Wallace, & Spencer, 2005). And the connection between socioeconomic status and Cerebral Palsy obviously means that non-Hispanic Blacks experience higher levels of Cerebral Palsy in the US than Caucasians (Yeargin-Allsopp et al., 2008). In light of the connections between low incomes and Cerebral Palsy, it is interesting that organizations representing people with this disability tend to advocate on issues such as health, education, disability discrimination legislation and employment (all of which are undoubtedly important), but tend not to advocate more broadly for income redistribution or other forms of social change designed to enhance the status of poor people.

Cerebral Palsy is only one of many disabilities associated with low incomes. There is also some evidence suggesting that socioeconomic problems increase the incidence of post-partum and antenatal depression among women. One study suggested that Black and Hispanic mothers were more likely to experience depression than Caucasian women. Some of the major factors contributing to this problem were lower income and financial hardship, as well as the higher incidence of poor pregnancies among women of color (Rich-Edwards et al., 2006). These findings are fairly consistent across the literature and confirm the need for maternal depression screening programs among poor women (Segre, O'Hara, Arndt, & Stuart, 2007). Moreover, they are an important reminder that "disability issues" are not necessarily distinct from "class issues" or "racial issues" – these three phenomena are often linked.

The association between mental illness and poverty is well known. However, this connection has often been couched in terms of two competing explanations: one emphasizing the ways in which living in poverty increases the risks of developing mental illness and another suggesting that having mental illness increases the risk of living in poverty (Hudson, 2005). There have been inconsistent, and somewhat competing, findings in the literature regarding this issue. This should not be surprising – couching such a complex and varied phenomena as 'mental illness' in terms of simple linear causes will obviously lead to inconsistent results. However, regardless of the cause, it is clear that a great number of people with mental illness live in poverty and experience higher rates of unemployment for much of their lives. Likewise, it is clear that many people of color experience both mental distress and some of the social causes of distress (such as poverty, discrimination, lack of affordable childcare, and unemployment). As a consequence, it behoves organizations representing people with mental illness to adopt a more active role in advocating around issues such as poverty, wages and taxation (as well as anti-discrimination, social inclusion and disability-specific issues).

The research on socioeconomic status and Intellectual Disability is fascinating – not only because it confirms the link between lower socioeconomic status and this disability, but also because it suggests that because of various prejudicial responses to disability, adults with intellectual disabilities are at even higher risk of poverty, unemployment, social isolation and crime victimization. Such prejudicial responses, on top of a life that is often lived in poverty, increase the incidence of emotional and behavioral problems and poorer physical health (Emerson, 2007). Once again, the failure of organizations representing people with intellectual disabilities to advocate around economic issues seems questionable.

A link between low socioeconomic status and Asthma is also evident. A meta-analysis of literature on asthma and socioeconomic status found that low socioeconomic status is an important determinant of lung function – even after adjusting for factors such as 'race', occupational exposure and smoking status (Hegewald & Crapo, 2007). Localized studies outline these findings in more detail. For instance, a study conducted in the Boston area found a strong correlation between socioeconomic status (measured by highest level of education, residence in a high or low poverty area and level of income) and asthma prevalence (Litonjua, Carey, Weiss, & Gold, 1999). Of course, it is important in any discussion of asthma to recognize its racial/ethnic dimensions:

asthma is twice as common, and morbidity rates are also much higher, for African Americans as opposed to Caucasians. As a result, there has been a debate over whether this higher mortality rate is due to cultural factors or socioeconomic factors. However, many studies conclude that while both 'race' and socioeconomic status are associated with higher risks of asthma, socioeconomic factors account for a large proportion of racial/ethnic differences in asthma prevalence rates (Litonjua et al., 1999).

Another area where the link between socioeconomic status and illness is evident is the case of cardiovascular diseases. One study of women with chest pain found a 250% higher all-cause mortality rate among women with a lower socioeconomic status, measured in terms of annual household income less than $20,000 (Rutledge et al., 2003). This study found a strong connection between mortality and lower socioeconomic status, even controlling for such factors as the severity of coronary artery disease, age, menopause status, and the use of hormone replacement therapy. People who had a lower socioeconomic status generally experienced higher levels of stress, fewer social and interpersonal resources, and more difficulties accessing the healthcare system (Rutledge et al., 2003).

Some studies focus on neighborhood poverty levels as a marker of socioeconomic status in order to estimate the risks associated with living in poor communities. One such study suggests that living in a poorer neighborhood (defined as one with at least 20% of the population below the poverty line) increases the risk of death (from all causes) by 13% in men and by 3% in women. It also states that five-year cancer survival rates were 10% lower in these poorer neighborhoods (Ward et al., 2004). A former Director of the US National Cancer Institute is alleged to have once commented "poverty is a carcinogen."

The review of the connections between adolescent health and socioeconomic status which has been conducted by Bradley and Corwyn is one of the best available (Bradley & Corwyn, 2002). They point out that socioeconomic status begins affecting people before they are even born: poorer people are more likely to experience growth retardation in-utero; and they are more likely to have a low birth weight, develop a disability, experience fetal alcohol syndrome, or to have what is commonly called "birth defects". Low socioeconomic status is associated with increased likelihood of injury and death, as well as higher risk of a number of disabilities at birth, such as sensory disabilities, stunted growth and lead poisoning. As well, when a child is premature, and lives the first three years in poverty, he or she is much more likely to develop problems in growth, health status, and neurological problems. And childhood poverty also has a great influence on later cognitive development - though its influence diminishes with age (Bradley & Corwyn, 2002). Also, there are a number of higher environmental risks which poor, young children experience as well, including inadequate nutrition, exposure to tobacco smoke, and inadequate health care access.

The experience of poverty either in early childhood or in adolescence can have long-term effects because it can make a person more vulnerable for later diseases or disabilities. For instance, people who experienced childhood/adolescence poverty are likely to experience higher blood pressure later in life. The development of mental problems in adolescence is also influenced by socioeconomic status. These associations are different for different types of psychiatric illnesses and unhealthy behaviors. For instance, maladaptive coping strategies and increased depression are more likely among young people from a poor socioeconomic background, but there have been inconsistent findings about the relationship between low socioeconomic status and substance abuse.

Bradley and Corwyn suggest that low socioeconomic status influences the ways in which people can access resources, namely: nutrition, health care, housing, and educationally stimulating materials. Also, parenting styles are different between people from lower socioeconomic backgrounds and those from wealthier backgrounds. Socioeconomic status also affects teacher expectations. Similarly, being from a poorer socioeconomic status also increases the amount of stress an individual experiences.

As Bradley and Corwyn note, research is needed to examine the ways in which particular risk factors (for instance, exposure to drugs) might be influenced, and mediated, by socioeconomic status. Mediating factors are important because they help us understand why two people can have the same socioeconomic status, but have different risk and protective factors, so the individuals go on completely different life courses. Some of these mediating factors include:

- Belief in personal control;
- Being optimistic;
- Social support;
- Self-esteem;
- Humor;
- Coping strategies;
- Communication skills;
- Family characteristics such as cohesion and shared values; and
- Availability of external support systems.

There are other qualifications that need to be made to this data. First, while it is possible to identify overall risks for a sub-population in terms of developing a range of disabilities, health conditions and illnesses, it is not possible to predict how this will influence any particular individual. Furthermore, it is important to remember that although many disabilities are connected to socioeconomic status, there are other disabilities which are not related to socioeconomic status. Additionally, because people have many identities, it is difficult to separate the influence of socioeconomic status from other factors that might put people at risk. For instance, some other social experiences that people have might put them at risk — such as 'race', ethnicity, single parenthood, living in particular neighborhoods, exposure to environmental toxins, and so on. Sorting out what is the particular influence of "socioeconomic status" aside from other issues is very difficult.

Additionally, many people believe that a higher socioeconomic status automatically benefits a child's development, as a result of having more resources and also as a result of the social connections which their parents can provide for them. There is some evidence that such benefits might not occur automatically, however. For instance, this connection might not occur for any of the following groups: people who have a high socioeconomic status, but live in rural communities which have less overall resources; people who have a high socioeconomic status who have recently migrated; people who have a high socioeconomic status but have experienced personal catastrophes; and people who have a high socioeconomic status from a minority culture. In terms of sociological analysis, this is an important reminder that the benefits of class and socioeconomic status are not distributed evenly, even among relatively privileged groups.

Unfortunately, although a great deal of attention has been directed towards establishing the connection between lower socioeconomic status and illness/disability, it is less commonly recognized that higher socioeconomic status also greatly reduces the chances of developing most illnesses, diseases and disabilities. One study exploring this topic examined whether a gradient in disability exists in the United States among persons with middle-class and upper-class incomes. This study found that socioeconomic privilege continues to have health benefits (and reduces the incidence of illness and disability) throughout the upper ranges of the socioeconomic hierarchy (Minkler et al., 2006). The higher incidence of illnesses and disabilities among people from lower socioeconomic backgrounds is commonly assumed to be related to poor nutrition, crowded conditions or and inadequate medical care. However, such experiences are not relevant to those in higher social status – and alternative explanations have been necessary to explain the (apparently) hidden health benefits of class and privilege.

Despite these qualifications, it is clear that lower socioeconomic status is strongly connected to problems of illness, disability and poor health. Such problems are further compounded by lack of access to the health care system. This connection between lower socioeconomic status and disability virtually demands that disability organizations broaden their agendas to include a specific focus on economic issues.

BARRIERS IN THE HEALTHCARE SYSTEM

Lack of access to health care is a major barrier which is influenced by socioeconomic status. Health care access is widely seen as being fundamental to efforts to reduce health inequalities associated with socioeconomic status. Not only does lack of health care access increase the vulnerability of people to various disabilities, diseases and illnesses, the provision of such health care greatly enhances overall wellness (Andrulis, 1998). Some indicators of the importance of health insurance include:

- People who are uninsured are more likely to receive insufficient healthcare and, even then, to receive such care late (Institute of Medicine, 2002);
- Uninsured people are more likely to report that they could not see a physician when needed because of cost issues (Leiyu, 2005);
- Lack of health care insurance is associated with lack of preventative and early detection measures (Rodríguez, Ward, & Pérez-Stable, 2005);
- People who are uninsured are more likely to be dead on admission to hospital and also are more likely to die in hospital (Leiyu, 2005); and
- Uninsured children are more likely to report an unmet need for assistance with hearing, vision, and mobility aids (Dusing, Skinner, & Mayer, 2004).

People with lower socioeconomic status not only report MUCH lower rates of health care insurance, they also report *different health-seeking behaviors*. For instance, Leiyu states that people who earn more than $50,000 per year are more likely to attend a physician's office rather than clinics or the emergency department; and people who earn less than $10,000 per are much more likely to go to the emergency department or clinics (Leiyu, 2005).

Also, people from lower socioeconomic backgrounds *wait longer* in seeking healthcare than those who come from higher socioeconomic status. Other barriers to healthcare access identified by Leiyu included that people from lower socioeconomic backgrounds having a long time to travel to their health care center, having no insurance, having to wait for a long time when scheduling appointments, and waiting for long periods in healthcare offices. People from lower socioeconomic status experienced these barriers at higher rates than those from higher socioeconomic backgrounds. People from lower socioeconomic backgrounds also tend to report higher levels of *dissatisfaction* with their health care.

Leiyu also states that people from lower socioeconomic backgrounds also have *less access to preventative services*:

- Mothers from lower socioeconomic backgrounds are less likely to receive prenatal care;
- Overall, women from lower socioeconomic backgrounds have less Pap smears and less mammograms;
- Men and women from lower socioeconomic backgrounds generally utilize a range of preventative services such as flu vaccinations, colon examination, bone densitometry, and lipid testing.
- Parents from lower socioeconomic backgrounds tend to report less guidance from physicians regarding the following topics: breast feeding, sleeping positions (to prevent Sudden Infant Death Syndrome), injury prevention, etc.
- People from lower socioeconomic backgrounds have higher rates of preventable hospitalizations as a result of conditions like asthma, diabetes and congestive heart failure.

Because they miss out on preventative opportunities, people from lower socioeconomic status may miss opportunities for earlier detection of health care problems.

Another important issue raised by Leiyu is that people from lower socioeconomic backgrounds often experience *physician bias and stereotyping*. They report the findings of one study that indicated physicians tend to regard people from lower socioeconomic backgrounds as less independent, responsible, rational, and intelligent than people from higher socioeconomic backgrounds. Such attitudes are likely to influence patient-doctor interactions. One example of such prejudice is that physicians are much less likely to refer women from lower socioeconomic backgrounds for a mammogram if they assume the woman cannot afford it and if they believe that she will not comply with doctor's orders (Leiyu, 2005).

The increased influence of *managed care programs in public insurance programs* such as Medicaid and Medicare are also identified by Leiyu as a problematic aspect of healthcare for people from lower socioeconomic status. These managed health care programs have been criticized for reducing patient autonomy, as well as restricting the range of options of physicians by cost-control measures.

In "Health Work with the Poor: A Practical Guide" (Keifer, 2000), a number of problems with the Medicaid system are identified:

- Only half of US families with incomes below the poverty line are eligible for Medicaid, and even those who are eligible face problems;
- A majority of physicians either do not accept Medicaid payments for services or restrict the number of Medicaid patients in their practice.
- Some studies suggest that Medicaid recipients have more advanced illness at diagnosis or hospital admission than privately insured patients.

Keifer suggests that there is a need for community action, to ensure better access to resources – education, housing, jobs, family and community supports – which would reduce the vulnerability of people from lower socioeconomic status. As well, Keifer recommends better training for health professionals in tailoring services to poor clients and targeting low-income patients in health education and preventative services (Keifer, 2000).

A very interesting 2005 book called "Minority Populations and Health: An Introduction to Health Disparities in the United States" suggests that addressing the impact of the uneven distribution of wealth has also been recognized as an important factor in health policy, but has not been given sufficient attention:

> In the United States there have been some policies directed at addressing the distribution of wealth. And there have been some efforts to provide persons of low socioeconomic status with resources that help to counterbalance their low SES (such as the earned income tax credit, the Section 8 housing program, food stamps, and Medicaid). Such programs are major components of the US welfare state. However, they are not substantial enough to be a sufficient counterweight to the debilitating effects on health of low SES (LaVeist, 2005).

LaVeist emphasizes that in addressing healthcare disparities, it is necessary to think about interventions on multiple levels. He identifies three levels of interventions – socioenvironmental, individual and system-level. While you may not agree with every component of these recommendations, or how they could be implemented (for instance, there are many different opinions about how to provide universal health care access), it is nevertheless useful to be thinking about each of these levels. LaVeist suggests that socioenvironmental changes could include community redevelopment, job creation, improved housing, the elimination of environmental hazards, and so on. Changes in the health care system advocated by LaVeist include increasing the availability of health care services, providing universal access to health care and pharmaceuticals, and increasing the number of providers who can speak a second language. Individual-level changes might include improved health literacy, healthy eating, the reduction or elimination of alcohol and drugs, increased health screenings, and so on.

LaVeist also identifies three specific areas where access to care can be improved:

Level One: Improving access to the health care system (addressing problems such as difficulty getting care, delays in care because of costs, and transportation problems);

Level Two: Addressing structural barriers within the system (such as difficulties getting appointments, difficulties getting advice after hours, and completing referrals to specialists); and

Level Three: Improving the ability of the provider to address patients' needs (such as improving trust so that they can become more aware of patients' conditions and functional limitations, improving clinician's cultural competence, and so on).

This idea of improving access to essential health care services is at the core of most recommendations for changing the health care system in the US today.

CONCLUSION

This chapter has discussed some aspects of the very complex relationship between socioeconomic status and disability. It begun by recognizing that there are different approaches to the question of wealth/income/poverty and illness. One tradition, heavily influenced by Marxist approaches, uses the term "social class" to describe the connections between relative deprivation and illness. Another tradition, influenced by Weberian approaches, has preferred the term "socioeconomic status". However, with the advent of more sophisticated approaches to inequality, such as Eric Olin Wright's innovative combination of Marxist and Weberian approaches, the gulf between these two schools of thought is not nearly as wide as once thought. The chapter explored an article by Corwin and Bradley on the connections between socioeconomic status and disability partly because it explicitly relied on Eric Olin Wright's theories of class in modernity.

Another important element of this chapter has been the reiteration of a strong connection between poverty and illness/disease/disability. This connection is undeniable – from the uterus to the grave, poorer people are at higher risk for developing many more diseases, disabilities and illnesses. Also, particular workplace experiences, and particular occupations, face additional health risks associated with workplace practices and environmental hazards. The chapter contained many examples of disabilities which are more concentrated among people from lower socioeconomic backgrounds, including Cerebral Palsy, Depression, Asthma, Intellectual Disability, and many more.

Inequalities in the distribution of health and illness are further compounded by lack of access to healthcare. The chapter identified a number of barriers in the health care system, including lack of insurance, lack of access to preventative services, physician bias and stereotyping, and problems with both managed care and Medicaid.

Overall, the evidence in this chapter is clear: socioeconomic status is intimately tied to a person's health, illness and disability experiences, and it may be further compounded by structural barriers within the healthcare system such as problems with Medicaid or managed care programs. In terms of the overall argument of the book, the chapter is an important reminder that particular forms of inequality and diversity – in this case, socioeconomic position – can shape people's illness and disability experiences in profound ways. Of course, no individual simply carries around one identity, such as socioeconomic status. Everyone is simultaneously gendered, sexualized, racialized, and so on. So the evidence in this chapter must be read in conjunction with the other chapters, in order to get a more comprehensive picture of the overlapping – and sometimes contradictory – ways in which both inequality manifests itself in the health and wellness of people in the US.

Chapter 5

CONCLUSION

Disability occurs alongside multiple other identities (such as sexuality, 'race' and ethnicity, socioeconomic status, etc.) – so it is a mistake to assume that it is the single most important identity of an individual. Indeed, a great deal of disability activism has been aimed at debunking the myth that disability is a 'master status'. However... identity politics around disability has tended to downplay, ignore or underestimate the diversity of people who may be identified as 'disabled'. This book is one intervention aimed at reminding those who might forget this diversity. Disability is always a sexed, gendered, racialized, ethnicized, and classed experience (just to name a few) ... and every response to disability operates within a framework of multilayered and complex patterns of inequality and identities. Every response to disability – whether it involves an attempt to dismantle a disabling barrier, or simply to develop some sense of commonality among people with various impairments, or even simply organizing a meeting for people with a particular impairment – occurs against this backdrop of inequality.

Chapter One highlighted the ways in which different disabilities are unevenly distributed according to various factors including geographic location, age, and so on. Chapters Two, Three and Four highlighted three more areas of different where disability is unevenly distributed – ethnicity, sex, and socioeconomic position. Chapter Two highlighted the way in which different ethnic groups face higher risks of certain diseases, disorders and disabilities, such as Multiple Sclerosis, Cystic Fibrosis, Migraine, and Mental Illness. Chapter Three demonstrated that many disabilities were unevenly distributed according to sex – including Post Traumatic Stress Disorder, Stroke, Migraine, Chronic Obstructive Pulmonary Disease, and Bipolar Disorder. Chapter Three also demonstrated some of the ways in which gender helps produce certain forms of disability. For instance, the chapter discussed how one impairment (Carpel Tunnel Syndrome) can be created through the gendered allocation of work and how other impairments such as Traumatic Brain Injury or Spinal Cord Injury can be the result of risky behaviors associated with certain forms of masculinity.

Chapter Four highlighted the uneven distribution of disability according to socioeconomic status. It demonstrated that throughout the life course, poorer people faced a much higher risk of developing a disability, illness or disease. Conversely, people from higher socioeconomic backgrounds consistently reported better overall levels of health and lower rates of disability than their poorer counterparts. The increased incidence of disability among poorer people is compounded by the presence of a number of barriers within the healthcare system, ranging from problems with Medicare and managed care programs to physician bias and stereotyping.

Each of these chapters should be read in conjunction with each other – every disabled person has a sex, an ethnicity, and a socioeconomic position – and disability may occur against a backdrop of simultaneous disadvantage in one or more of these areas. More broadly, disability studies has only just begun to analyze the ways in which disability and other forms of inequality are implicated in certain forms of power, normativity, and marginalization within modernity. The recent engagement of disability studies scholars with literature from the fields of postcolonialism and queer theory, for instance, is an important development because it broadens the discussion to address power and the body more generally and questions some of the essentialism associated with identity politics (Sherry, 2004, 2007). Engagement with these postmodern discourses shifts the discussion away from the ways in which disabled people are a minority group and instead focuses on the ways in which certain bodies are constructed in medical, legal, social, educational and economic discourse at the same time as they are manifested materially in the body, mind and senses. By exploring the operation of power on the body more generally, it is possible to suggest connections between disabled bodies and other sorts of bodies which might be ignored in a more narrow 'minority model' approach.

There are many books within disability studies which have marginalized questions of 'race', ethnicity, sex, gender, and class – unfortunately assuming that these issues are only relevant to a minority of disabled people. This (implicit, usually unarticulated) additive model of identity is deeply problematicfor a number of reasons:

- It relegates issues of sexism, racism, and other forms of discrimination to the side (as if they are not deeply involved in making some groups more susceptible to disability than others); and
- It ignores the ways in which various forms of power such as normalization, marginalization and social exclusion intersect and overlap and are involved in the production and regulation of bodies in many social contexts (not just disabled bodies, but also aged, racialized, sexualized, ethnicized, and classed bodies).

The aim of this book was to broaden the discussion of disability in order to highlight the influence of various forms of social inequality such as ethnicity, gender and socioeconomic status. Disability is not experienced in a social vacuum – and some people face higher risks of developing a disability than others. Furthermore, there are gendered, racialized and classed barriers in various responses to disability. 'Race', ethnicity, sex, gender, social class… these are not side-issues in the study of disability. The connection between such forms of inequality and the production and regulation of bodies must actually become central to disability studies.

REFERENCES

Altman, B. M., Barnartt, S. N., Hendershot, G., & Larson, S. (Eds.). (2003). *Using Survey Data to Study Disability: Results from the National Health Interview Survey on Disability*. Oxford, UK: Elsevier.

Andrulis, D. P. (1998). Access to Care Is the Centerpiece in the Elimination of Socioeconomic Disparities in Health *Annals of Internal Medicine, 129*(5), 412-416.

Artazcoz, L., Borrell, C., Cortàs, I., Escribà-Agüir, V., & Cascant, L. (2007). Occupational epidemiology and work related inequalities in health: a gender perspective for two complementary approaches to work and health research. *Journal of Epidemiology and Community Health 61*(Supplement 2), ii39-ii45.

Bagatell, N. (2007). Orchestrating voices: autism, identity and the power of discourse. *Disability and Society, 22*(4), 413-426.

Barlow, T. E. (2005). Eugenic Woman, Semicolonialism, and Colonial Modernity as Problems for Postcolonial Theory. In A. Loomba, S. Kaul, M. Bunzl & A. Burton (Eds.), *Postcolonial Studies and Beyond* (pp. 359-384). Durham, NC: Duke University Press.

Barnes, C., Mercer, G., & Shakespeare, T. (2005). *Exploring Disability: A Sociological Introduction*. Cambridge, UK: Polity Press.

Baruffi, G., Hardy, C. J., Waslien, C. L., Uyehara, S. J., & Krupitsky, D. (2004). Ethnic differences in the prevalence of overweight among young children in Hawaii. *Journal of the American Dietetic Association, 104*(11), 1701-1707.

Bickel, J., Croft, K. and Marshall, R. (1996). *Enhancing the Environment for Women in Academic Medicine*. Washington, DC: Association of American Medical Colleges.

Blackless, M., Charuvastra, A., Derryck, A., Fausto-Sterling, A., Lauzanne, K., & Lee, E. (2000). How Sexually Dimorphic Are We? Review and Synthesis. *American Journal of Human Biology, 12*, 151-166.

Blackman, D. J., & Masi, C. M. (2006). Racial and Ethnic Disparities in Breast Cancer Mortality: Are We Doing Enough to Address the Root Causes? *Journal of Clinical Oncology, 24*(14), 2170-2178.

Blanchard, J., & Hosek, S. (2003). *Financing Health Care for Women with Disabilities*. Santa Monica, CA: Rand Health for FISA Foundation.

Bonilla-Silva, E. (2006). *Racism without Racists: Color-Blind Racism and the Persistence of Racial Inequality in the United States* (2nd ed.). Lanham MD Rowman & Littlefield Publishers, Inc.

Boynton-Jarrett, R., Rich-Edwards, J., Malspeis, S., Missmer, S. A., & Wright, R. (2005). A Prospective Study of Hypertension and Risk of Uterine Leiomyomata. *American Journal of Epidemiology, 161* (7), 628-638.

Bradley, R. H., & Corwyn, R. F. (2002). Socioeconomic Status and Child Development. *Annual Review of Psychology, 53*, 371-399.

Carrie, D. M., & Chan, N. K.-C. (2008). Celiac disease in North America: the disabling experience. *Disability and Society, 23*(1), 89-96.

Chang, A. M., Mumma, B., Sease, K. L., Robey, J. L., Shofer, F. S., & Hollander, J. E. (2007). Gender Bias in Cardiovascular Testing Persists after Adjustment for Presenting Characteristics and Cardiac Risk. *Academic Emergency Medicine, 14*(7), 599-605.

Chen, M. S. (2005). Cancer health disparities among Asian Americans: What we know and what we need to do *Cancer, 104*(12), 2895-2902.

Cintron, A., & Morrison, R. S. (2006). Pain and Ethnicity in the United States: A Systematic Review. *Journal of Palliative Medicine, 9*(6), 1454-1473.

Connell, R. W. (2005). *Masculinities* (2nd ed.). Abingdon, UK: Polity Press.

Conrad, P. (2007). *The Medicalization of Society*. Baltimore, MD: The Johns Hopkins University Press.

Correa-de-Araujo, R., Stevens, B., Moy, E., Nilasena, D., Chesley, F., & McDermott, K. (2006). Gender differences across racial and ethnic groups in the quality of care for acute myocardial infarction and heart failure associated with comorbidities. *Women's Health Issues, 16*(2), 44-55.

Courtenay, W. H. (2000). Constructions of Masculinity and their influence on men's wellbeing: a theory of gender and health. *Social Science & Medicine, 50*(10), 1385-1401.

Czlonkowska, A., Ciesielska, A., Gromadzka, G., & Kurkowska-Jastrzebska, I. (2005). Estrogen and Cytokines Production - The Possible Cause of Gender Differences in Neurological Diseases *Current Pharmaceutical Design, 11*(8), 1017-1030.

Deal, M. (2003). Disabled People's Attitudes toward Other Impairment Groups: A Hierarchy of Impairments. *Disability and Society, 18*(7), 897-910.

Dept. of Health and Human Services, U. S. P. H. S. (1999). *Mental health : A Report of the Surgeon General.* Washington, D.C.

Development, N. I. o. C. H. a. H. (2000). *Health Disparities: Bridging the Gap.* Retrieved.   from http://www.nichd.nih.gov/publications/pubs/upload/health_disparities.pdf.

Di Marcoa, F., Vergaa, F., Reggentea, M., Casanovaa, F. M., Santusa, P., Blasib, F., et al. (2006). Anxiety and depression in COPD patients: The roles of gender and disease severity. *Respiratory Medicine 100*(10), 1767-1774.

Diez Roux, A. V. (2004). Estimating neighborhood health effects: the challenges of causal inference in a complex world. *Social Science and Medicine, 54*(10), 1953 1960.

Ditunno, J. F., & Formal, C. S. (1994). Chronic Spinal Cord Injury. *New England Journal of Medicine, 330*(8), 550-556.

Dusing, S. C., Skinner, A. C., & Mayer, M. L. (2004). Unmet need for therapy services, assistive devices, and related services: data from the National Survey of Children With Special Health Care Needs. *Ambulatory Pediatrics 4*, 448-454.

Duster, T. (2003). *Backdoor to Eugenics.* New York, NY: Routledge.

Emerson, E. (2007). Poverty and People with Intellectual Disabilities. *Mental Retardation And Developmental Disabilities Research Reviews, 13*(2), 107-113.

Farmer, P. (1993). *AIDS and Accusation: Haiti and the Geography of Blame.* . Berkeley, CA: University of California Press.

Ferrary, E., & Jablonski, R. A. S. (2004). Common Medical Problems: Cardiovascular through Hematological Disorders. In E. Q. Youngkin & M. S. Davis (Eds.), *Women's Health: A Primary Care Clinical Guide* (pp. 679-750). Upper Sadle River, NJ: Pearson Prentice Hall.

Galdas, P. M., Cheater, F., & Marshall, P. (2005). Men and health help-seeking behaviour: literature review. *Journal of Advanced Nursing, 49*(6), 616-623.

Gibson, P. R., & Lindberg, A. (2007). Work accommodation for people with multiple chemical sensitivity *Disability and Society, 22*(7), 717-732.

Gilman, S. (1985). *Difference and Pathology: Stereotypes of Sexuality, Race and Madness.* Ithica, NY: Cornell University Press.

Gleicher, N., & Barad, D. H. (2007). Gender as risk factor for autoimmune diseases. *Journal of Autoimmunity, 28*(1), 1-6.

Gomberg, E. S. L. (1988). Alcoholic Women in Treatment: The Question of Stigma and Age. *Alcohol and Alcoholism, 23*(6), 507-514.

Gorman, B. K., & Read, J. n. G. (2006). Gender Disparities in Adult Health: An Examination of Three Measures of Morbidity. *Journal of Health and Social Behavior, 47* (2), 95–110.

Green-Hennessy, S. (2002). Factors Associated With Receipt of Behavioral Health Services Among Persons With Substance Dependence. *Psychiatric Services, 53*(12), 1592-1598.

Groce, N. E. (2006). *Everyone Here Spoke Sign Language.* Harvard, MA: Harvard University Press.

Han, M. K., Postma, D., Mannino, D. M., Giardino, N. D., Buist, S., Curtis, J. L., et al. (2007). Gender and Chronic Obstructive Pulmonary Disease: Why It Matters. *American Journal of Respiratory and Critical Care Medicine, 176*(10), 1179-1184.

Hegewald, M. J., & Crapo, R. O. (2007). Socioeconomic Status and Lung Function. *Chest, 132*(5), 1608-1614

Hill Collins, P. (2006). *From Black Power to Hip Hop.* Philadelphia, PA: Temple University Press.

Howard, G., Labarthe, D. R., Hu, J., Yoon, S., & Howard, V. J. (2007). Regional Differences in African Americans' High Risk for Stroke: The Remarkable Burden of Stroke for Southern African Americans. *Annals of Epidemiology, 17*(9), 689-696.

Hudson, C. G. (2005). Socioeconomic Status and Mental Illness: Tests of the Social Causation and Selection Hypotheses. *American Journal of Orthopsychiatry, 75*(1), 3-18.

Institute of Medicine. (2002). Care Without Coverage: Too Little, Too Late. Retrieved May 6, 2008, from http://www.iom.edu/Object.File/Master/4/160/Uninsured2FINAL.pdf

Karner, C. (2007). *Ethnicity and Everyday Life.* New York, NY: Routledge.

Keifer, C. (2000). *Health Work with the Poor: A Practical Guide.* New Brunswick, NJ: Rutgers University Press.

Kerem, B., Chiba-Falek, O., Kerem E. (1997). Cystic fibrosis in Jews: frequency and mutation distribution. *Genetic Testing, 1*(1), 35-39.

Kerr, A., & Shakespeare, T. (2002). *Genetic Politics: From Eugenics to Human Genome.* Cheltenham (Eng.) New Clarion Press.

Kines, P., Hannerz, H., Mikkelsen, K. L., & Tüchsen, F. (2006). Industrial sectors with high risk of women's hospital-treated injuries. *American Journal of Industrial Medicine, 50*(1), 13-21.

Kissela, B. M., Khoury, J., Kleindorfer, D., Woo, D., Schneider, A., Alwell, K., et al. (2005). Epidemiology of Ischemic Stroke in Patients With Diabetes: The Greater Cincinnati/Northern Kentucky Stroke Study *Diabetes Care, 28*, 355-359.

Krishnan, V., & Collop, N. A. (2006). Gender differences in sleep disorders. *Current Opinion in Pulmonary Medicine, 12*(6), 383-389.

Kurtzke, J. F., Beebe, G. W., & Norman, J. E. J. (1979). Epidemiology of multiple sclerosis in U.S. veterans: 1. Race, sex, and geographic distribution. *Neurology, 29*(9 Pt 1), 1228-1235.

Labiche, L., Chan, W., Saldin, K. R., & Morgenstern, L. B. (2002). Sex and acute stroke presentation. *Annals of Emergency Medicine, 40*(5), 453–460.

Lane, N. E. (2006). Epidemiology, etiology, and diagnosis of osteoporosis *American Journal of Obstetrics and Gynecology, 194*(2), S3-S11

Lau, E. M. C. (2001). Epidemiology of osteoporosis. *Best Practice, 15*(3), 335-344.

LaVeist, T. A. (2005). *Minority Populations and Health: An Introduction to Health Disparities in the United States*. San Francisco, CA: Jossey-Bass.

Leibenluft, E. (1996). Women with bipolar illness: clinical and research issues. *American Journal of Psychiatry, 153* 163-173. .

Leiyu, S. (2005). *Vulnerable Populations in the United States*. San Francisco, CA: Jossey-Bass.

Linton, S. (1998). *Claiming Disability: Knowledge and Identity*. New York, NY: New York University Press.

Lipsitz, G. (2006). *The Possessive Investment in Whiteness*. Philadelphia, PA: Temple University Press.

Litonjua, A. A., Carey, V. J., Weiss, S. T., & Gold, D. R. (1999). Race, Socioeconomic Factors, and Area of Residence Are Associated With Asthma Prevalence. *Pediatric Pulmonology, 28*, 394–401.

Longmore, P. K. (2003). *Why I Burned My Book and Other Essays on Disability*. Philadelphia, PA: Temple University Press.

Machado, M.-C. L., Krishnan, J. A., Buist, S. A., Bilderback, A. L., Fazolo, G. P., Santarosa, M. G., et al. (2006). Gender Differences on Survival in Oxygen-dependent Chronic Obstructive Pulmonary Disease Patients. *American Journal of Respiratory and Critical Care Medicine, 174*(5), 524-529.

McDiarmida, M., Olivera, M., Ruserb, J., & Gucera, P. (2000). Male and Female
    Rate Differences in Carpal Tunnel Syndrome Injuries: Personal Attributes or
    Job Tasks? *Environmental Research, 83*(1), 23-32.

Mendelsohn, M. E., & Karas, R. H. (2005). Molecular and Cellular Basis of
    Cardiovascular Gender Differences *Science, 308*(5728), 1583 - 1587.

Mensah, G. A., Mokdad, A. H., Ford, E. S., Greenlund, K. J., & Croft, J. B.
    (2005). State of Disparities in Cardiovascular Health in the United States.
    Circulation, 111(10), 1233-1241.

Michalko, R. (2002). *The Difference That Disability Makes.* Philadelphia, PA:
    Temple University Press.

Minkler, M., Fuller-Thomson, E., & Guralnik, J. M. (2006). Gradient of Disability
    across the Socioeconomic Spectrum in the United States. *New England
    Journal of Medicine, 355,* 695-703.

Mitchell, S., & Schlesinger, M. (2005). Managed Care and Gender Disparities in
    Problematic Health Care Experiences. *Health Services Research, 40*(5 Pt.1),
    1489–1513. .

Mock, J., McPhee, S. J., Nguyen, T., Wong, C., Doan, H., Lai, K. Q., et al.
    (2007). Effective Lay Health Worker Outreach and Media-Based Education
    for Promoting Cervical Cancer Screening Among Vietnamese American
    Women. *American Journal of Public Health, 97*(9), 1693-1700.

Morgan, W. J., Butler, S. M., Johnson, C. A., Colin, A. A., FitzSimmons, S. C.,
    Geller, D. E., et al. (1999). Epidemiologic Study of Cystic Fibrosis: Design
    and Implementation of a Prospective, Multicenter, Observational Study of
    Patients With Cystic Fibrosis in the U.S. and Canada. *Pediatric Pulmonology,
    28,* 231–241.

Morrell, M. J., & Flynn, K. (Eds.). (2003). *Women with Epilepsy: A Handbook of
    Health and Treatment Issues.* Cambridge, UK: Cambridge University Press.

Naismith, R. T., Trinkaus, K., & Cross, A. H. (2006). Phenotype and prognosis in
    African-Americans with multiple sclerosis: a retrospective chart review.
    Multiple Sclerosis, 12(6), 775-781.

National Center for PTSD. (2005). *Epidemiological Facts about PTSD.* Retrieved.
    from.

Neckerman, K. M., & Torche, F. (2007). Inequality: Causes and Consequences.
    Annual Review of Sociology, 33, 335-357.

Nelson, A. L., Fragala, G., & Menzel, N. N. (2006). Myths and Facts about Back
    Injuries in Nursing. In A. Nelson (Ed.), *Safe Patient Handling And
    Movement: A Guide for Nurses And Other Health Care Professionals* (pp. 27-
    40). New York, NY: Springer Publishing Company.

Nenner, R. P., Imperato, Pascal James, Silver, Alan L, Will, Theodore O. . (1994). Qualilty of Care Problems among Medicare and Medicaid Patients. *Journal of Community Health, Vol. 19*(5), 307-318.

O'Brien, R. (2004). Defining Moments: (Dis)ability, Individuality, and Normalcy. In R. Obrien (Ed.), *Voices from the edge: Narratives about the Americans with Disabilities Act* (pp. 40 - 52). New York, NY: Oxford University Press.

Odding, E., Roebroeck, M., & Stam, H. (2006). The epidemiology of cerebral palsy: Incidence, impairments and risk factors. *Disability and Rehabilitation, 28*(4), 181-191.

Oliver, M. (1990). *The Politics of Disablement*. London: Palgrave McMillan.

Oliver, M. (1996). *Understanding Disability: From Theory to Practice*. London: Macmillan.

Pálsson, G. (2007). *Anthropology and the New Genetics*. Cambridge: Cambridge University Press.

Percival, J., Hanson, J., & Osipovic, D. (2006). A positive outlook? The housing needs and aspirations of working age people with visual impairments. *Disability and Society, 21*(7), 661 675.

Priestley, M. (1999). *Disability Politics and Community Care*. London, UK: Jessica Kingsley Publishers.

PTSD, N. C. f. Epidemiological Facts about PTSD. Retrieved 12 December 2007, 2007, from http://www.ncptsd.va.gov/ncmain/ncdocs/fact_shts/fs_ epidemiological.html

Rademaker, M. (2001). Do Women Have More Adverse Drug Reactions? *American Journal of Clinical Dermatology, 2*(6), 349-351.

Read, J. n. G., & Gorman, B. K. (2006). Gender inequalities in US adult health: The interplay of race and ethnicity. *Social Science & Medicine, 62*(5), 1045-1065.

Rich-Edwards, J. W., Kleinman, K., Abrams, A., Harlow, B. L., McLaughlin, T. J., Joffe, H., et al. (2006). Sociodemographic predictors of antenatal and postpartum depressive symptoms among women in a medical group practice *Journal of Epidemiology and Community Health 60*, 221-227.

Rinker, J. R., Trinkaus, K., Naismith, R. T., & Cross, A. H. (2007). Higher IgG index found in African Americans versus Caucasians with multiple sclerosis. *Neurology, 69*(68-72).

Rioux, M. H., & Bach, M. (Eds.). (1994). *Disability is not Measles: New research paradigms in disability*. Ontario: Institut Roeher.

Rodríguez, M. A., Ward, L. M., & Pérez-Stable, E. J. (2005). Breast and Cervical Cancer Screening: Impact of Health Insurance Status, Ethnicity, and Nativity of Latinas. *Annals of Family Medicine, 3*, 235-241

Roquer, J., Campello, A. R., & Gomis, M. (2003). Sex Differences in First-Ever Acute Stroke *Stroke, 34*, 1581-1585.

Rosenfeld, D., & Faircloth, C. (Eds.). (2006). *Medicalized Masculinities.* Philadelphia, PA: Temple University Press.

Rothenberg, B. M., Pearson, T., Zwanziger, J., & Mukamel, D. (2004). Explaining disparities in access to high-quality cardiac surgeons. *The Annals of Thoracic Surgery, 78*, 18-24.

Ruland, S., Raman, R., Chaturvedi, S., Leurgans, S., Gorelick, P. B., & Investigators, f. t. A. (2003). Awareness, treatment, and control of vascular risk factors in African Americans with stroke. *Neurology, 60*, 64-68.

Russell, M. (1998). *Beyond Ramps: Disability at the End of the Social Contract.* Monroe, MA: Common Courage Press.

Rutledge, T., Reis, S. E., Olson, M., Owens, J., Kelsey, S. F., Pepine, C. J., et al. (2003). Socioeconomic Status Variables Predict Cardiovascular Disease Risk Factors and Prospective Mortality Risk Among Women With Chest Pain. *Behavior Modification, 27*(1), 54-67.

Schofield, T., Connell, R. W., Walker, L., Wood, J. F., & Butland, D. L. (2000). Understanding men's health and illness: a gender relations approach to policy, research and practice. *Journal of American College Health, 48*(6), 247-256.

Seedat, S., Stein, D. J., & Carey, P. D. (2005). Post-Traumatic Stress Disorder in Women: Epidemiological and Treatment Issues. *CNS Drugs, 19*(5), 411-427.

Segre, L. S., O'Hara, M. W., Arndt, S., & Stuart, S. (2007). The prevalence of postpartum depression: the relative significance of three social status indices *Social Psychiatry and Epidemiology, 42*(4), 316-321.

Shapiro, J. (1994). *No Pity: People with Disabilities Forging a New Civil Rights Movement.* New York, NY: Times Books, Random House.

Sherry, M. (2004). Overlaps and contradictions between queer theory and disability studies *Disability and Society, 19*(7), 769-783.

Sherry, M. (2006). *If I Only Had A Brain: Deconstructing Brain Injury.* New York, NY: Routledge.

Sherry, M. (2007). (Post)colonizing Disability. *Wagadu, 4.*

Sherry, M. (Ed.) (forthcoming-a) Encyclopedia of Cancer. Thousand Oaks, CA: Sage.

Sherry, M. (Ed.) (forthcoming-b) Encyclopedia of Disability History. Facts on File.

Shulman, L. M. (2007). Gender Differences in Parkinson's Disease. *Gender/Medicine, 4*(1), 8-18.

Siebers, T. (2006). Disability Studies and the Future of Identity Politics. In L. M. Alcoff, M. Hames-García, S. P. Mohanty & P. M. L. Moya (Eds.), *Identity Politics Reconsidered* (pp. 10-30). New York, NY: Palgrave McMillan.

Silverman, E. K., Weiss, S. T., Drazen, J. M., Chapman, H. A., Carey, V., Campbell, E. J., et al. (2000). Gender-Related Differences in Severe, Early-Onset Chronic Obstructive Pulmonary Disease. *American Journal of Respiratory and Critical Care Medicine, 162*(6), 2152-2158.

Singh, G. K., & Kogan, M. D. (2007). Widening Socioeconomic Disparities in US Childhood Mortality, 1969--2000. *American Journal of Public Health, 97*(9), 1658-1665.

Smedley, B., Stith, A., & Nelson, A. R. (Eds.). (2003). *Unequal Treatment: Confronting Racial and Ethnic Disparities in Health Care.* Washington, DC: Institute of Medicine of the National Academies.

Song, M. (2003). *Choosing Ethnic Identity.* Malden, MA: Blackwell.

Soriano, F. L., Rivera, L. M., Williams, K. J., Daley, S. P., & Reznik, V. M. (2004). Navigating between cultures: the role of culture in youth violence. *Journal of Adolescent Health, 34*(3), 169-176.

Spencer, A. P., & Wingate, S. (2005). Cardiovascular drug therapy in women. *Journal of Cardiovascular Nursing, 20*(6), 408-417.

Stansbury, J. P., Jia, H., Williams, L. S., Vogel, B., & Duncan, P. W. (2005). Ethnic disparities in stroke: epidemiology, acute care, and postacute outcomes. *Stroke, 36*(2), 374-386.

Stewart, W. F., Lipton, R. B., & Liberman, J. (1996). Variation in Migraine Prevalence by Race. *Neurology, Vol. 47*(1), 52-59.

Sue, S., & Chu, J. Y. (2003). The Mental Health of Ethnic Minority Groups: Challenges Posed by the Supplement to the Surgeon General's Report on Mental Health: The Politics of Science: Culture, Race, Ethnicity, and the Supplement to the Surgeon General's Report on Mental Health *Culture, Medicine and Psychiatry, 27*(4), 447-465.

Sundrum, R., Logan, S., Wallace, A., & Spencer, N. (2005). Cerebral palsy and socioeconomic status: a retrospective cohort study. *Archives of Disease in Childhood, 90*, 15-18.

Swain, J., Gillman, M., & French, S. (1998). *Confronting Disabling Barriers: Towards Making Organisations Accessible.* Birmingham: Venture Press.

Tamayo-Sarver, J. H., Hinze, S. W., Cydulka, R. K., & Baker, D. W. (2003). Racial and Ethnic Disparities in Emergency Department Analgesic Prescription. *American Journal of Public Health, 93*(12), 2067-2073.

Thom, B. (1986). Sex Differences in Help-seeking for Alcohol Problems-1. The Barriers to Help-seeking. *Addiction, 81*(6), 777-788.

Thom, T., Haase, N., Rosamond, W., Howard, V. J., Rumsfeld, J., Manolio, T., et al. (2006). Heart Disease and Stroke Statistics—2006 Update: A Report From the American Heart Association Statistics Committee and Stroke Statistics Subcommittee. *Circulation, 113*(6), e85-e151.

Thomas, C. (2001). Medicine, Gender and Disability: Disabled Women's Health Care Experiences. *Health Care for Women International, 22*(3), 245-262.

Thomasson, H. R. (1995). Gender Differences in Alcohol Metabolism: Physiological Responses to Ethanol. *Recent Developments in Alcoholism 12*, 163-179.

Thomson, R. G. (1997). *Extraordinary Bodies: Figuring Physical Disability in American Culture and Literature.* New York, NY: Columbia University Press.

Turrell, G., Hewitt, B., Patterson, C., & Oldenburg, B. (2003). Measuring socio-economic position in dietary research: is choice of socio-economic indicator important? *Public Health Nutrition, 6*(2), 191-200.

Wald, P. (2008). *Contagious: Cultures, Carriers, and the Outbreak Narrative.* Durham, NC: Duke University Press.

Ward, E., Jemal, A., Cokkinides, V., Singh, G. K., Cardinez, C., Ghafoor, A., et al. (2004). Cancer Disparities by Race/Ethnicity and Socioeconomic Status. *CA: A Cancer Journal for Clinicians, 54*, 78-93.

Waters, M. (1990). *Ethnic Options: Choosing Identities in America* Berkeley, CA: University of California Press. .

Weisner, C., & Schmidt, L. (1992). Gender disparities in treatment for alcohol problems. *Journal of the American Medical Association, 268*(14), 1872-1876.

Wilkinson, R. (2005). *The Impact of Inequality.* New York, NY: The New Press.

Williams, D. R., & Jackson, P. B. (2005). Social Sources Of Racial Disparities In Health *Health Affairs, 24*(2), 325-334.

Wizemann, T. M., & Pardue, M. L. (Eds.). (2001). *Exploring The Biological Contributions to Human Health: Does Sex Matter?* . Washington, DC: Committee on Understanding the Biology of Sex and Gender Differences Institute Of Medicine, National Academies Press.

Wright, E. O. (2000). *Class Counts: Student Edition.* New York, NY: Cambridge University Press.

Xue, Y., Leventhal, T., Brooks-Gunn, J., & Earls, F. J. (2005). Neighborhood Residence and Mental Health Problems of 5- to 11-Year-Olds. *Archives of General Psychiatry, 62*, 554-563.

Yeargin-Allsopp, M., Van Naarden Braun, K., Doernberg, N. S., Benedict, R. E., Kirby, R. S., & Durkin, M. S. (2008). Prevalence of Cerebral Palsy in 8-Year-Old Children in Three Areas of the United States in 2002: A Multisite Collaboration. *Pediatrics, 121*(3), 547-554.

Zimmermann, S. M. (1998). *Silicone Survivors: Women's Experiences with Breast Implants*. Philadelphia, PA: Temple University Press.

Index

D

E

F

O

N

P

Q